TRUTH REVEALED SERIES

SECRETS
OF THE RED CAPS
NORTHERN IRELAND

UNDISCLOSED MATERIAL
NEVER TOLD UNTIL NOW

Dedication

TO THE ROYAL MILITARY POLICE WHO SERVED IN NORTHERN IRELAND

This work is dedicated to the brave men and women of the Royal Military Police who served with distinction and courage in Northern Ireland during one of the most challenging periods in the region's history. Your unwavering commitment to duty, professionalism under pressure, and sacrifice in the pursuit of peace and security will not be forgotten.

To those who served and returned home, and to those who made the ultimate sacrifice, we honour your service and remember your dedication to protecting others in the most difficult of circumstances.

Their service, our gratitude. Their sacrifice, our remembrance.

Roll of Honour Northern Ireland

In memory of those who made the ultimate sacrifice

LCpl	Joliffe	W G	01 March 1971
Cpl	Holman	A J	11 February 1973
Sgt	Young	S	18 May 1973
Cpl	Lane	A R	30 May 1973
Cpl	Roberts	R J	30 May 1973
LCpl	Mundy	P C	20 February 1974
Cpl	Milne	S K	20 February 1974
Cpl	Lea	T F	21 January 1975
Cpl	Booth	J R	29 January 1975
Cpl	Hards	M R	17 April 1976
SSgt	Stryker	A S	4 June 1976
Cpl	Middlemas	G H	8 November 1977
Cpl	Snaith	W I	24 January 1979
Sgt	Ross	D	27 March 1984
Cpl	Hicks	T J	8/9 January 1989
LCpl	Chappell	D M	19 September 1991
Cpl	Bacon	P A	14/15 February 1992
LCpl	Melling	P	3 September 1997
Sgt	Stevenson	A	3 April 2004
WO1	Gemmell	S B	9 March 2005

Glossary

(In alphabetical order)

Catholic: A Catholic in Northern Ireland often refers to someone from the Roman Catholic or Nationalist/Republican community. This identity reflects cultural and social roots more than religious practice. Most identify as Nationalist, Republican, or Northern Irish.

Garda: An Garda Síochána is the national police force of the Republic of Ireland, comprising over 14,000 members – most of whom are believed to be Catholic. To date, they have not released an official breakdown of religious affiliation.

IRA: The Irish Republican Army (Óglaigh na hÉireann) was formed in 1919 to fight for Irish independence from Britain. After Ireland's partition in 1921, the IRA's influence declined. It resurfaced in 1969 during the Northern Ireland conflict, splitting into the Official and Provisional wings. The Official IRA declared a ceasefire in 1972, while the Provisional IRA continued its campaign until its final ceasefire in July 1997. In 2005, they surrendered their weapons.

Ireland (Irish - Éire): Ireland is an island made up of two political entities: the Republic of Ireland and Northern Ireland.

Many may be surprised to learn that Ireland was first inhabited around 1900 BC by Mesolithic hunter-gatherers. In 432 AD, Saint Patrick arrived from Britain and began converting the population to Christianity, especially in Ulster, where it replaced many pagan traditions.

By the 1600s, Ireland had become a battleground for Catholic and Protestant kings competing for power. While Catholicism was first introduced by Saint Patrick, the Protestant Reformation in the 16th century led many Catholic priests to convert to Protestantism.

Northern Ireland: Consists of six counties in the province of Ulster (nine counties), with Belfast as its capital. Established in 1921, it remains part of the United Kingdom and operates under a devolved government.

Before partition, Carrickfergus and Belfast were key entry points to the north, which had a larger Protestant population due to the Plantation under Elizabeth I. Many Protestants settled in the north, while others moved south, contributing skills that helped develop business and infrastructure.

The border was drawn based on community populations; Cavan and Donegal, despite having large Protestant populations, were included in the Republic to appease Catholics.

As of 2021, Northern Ireland's population was 1.9 million – 43.5% Protestant and 45.7% Catholic. Notably, 31.5% of a new generation now identify as Northern Irish, taking pride in their shared homeland.

Orange Order: The Orange Order, or Loyal Orange Association, was founded in 1795 as an Irish Protestant political society. Originally called the Orange Society, it was named in honour of Dutch Protestant William of Orange, who defeated the Catholic King James II in 1690.

Each year on July 12th, the Order commemorates this victory with parades, where over 30,000 members wear orange collarettes and march behind Protestant bands.

Protestant: Someone belonging to a Christian tradition that separated from the Roman Catholic Church during the Reformation. In Northern Ireland, they may or may not be active in the church, but typically identify as British or Northern Irish.

Republic of Ireland: Comprised of 26 counties with Dublin as its capital, the Republic was formed following the 1922 Anglo-Irish Treaty, initially as the Irish Free State with Dominion status. A new constitution in 1937 renamed it "Ireland," and in 1949, it was formally declared a republic.

The Taoiseach serves as head of government, and the president is a non-executive head of state. The Gaelicisation Policy made Irish language instruction compulsory in schools, affecting Protestant children and civil servants, some of whom lost jobs for not speaking Gaelic.

Although officially neutral in both World Wars, many Irish citizens fought alongside British forces. Upon returning, however, they were not publicly honoured, and the Second World War was excluded from school curricula until recent years. In 2021, the Republic's population was 5.01 million, with 80% identifying as Catholic.

RUC: Royal Ulster Constabulary served as Northern Ireland's police force from 1922 to 2001, peaking at 8,500 officers and 4,500 reservists. Viewed by the IRA as a symbol of British authority, the RUC operated as a heavily armed and militarised force, using submachine guns, armoured vehicles, and fortified stations.

Few Catholics joined, largely due to IRA intimidation in nationalist areas. Despite this, the RUC gained a global reputation for professionalism. During the Troubles, Republican terrorists caused nearly 9,000 injuries and 319 RUC deaths, making it the most dangerous police force in the world by 1983. In 2000, it was awarded the George Cross for bravery. It was replaced by the Police Service of Northern Ireland (PSNI) in 2001.

Glossary

Sinn Féin: Founded in 1905, Sinn Féin became politically aligned with the IRA in 1919. In 1970, it split into Official Sinn Féin (later the Workers Party) and Provisional Sinn Féin – the current party active in both Northern Ireland and the Republic.

The party has faced criticism due to some members, including councillors and MLAs, having past convictions for IRA-related activities, including murder and bombings. While Sinn Féin now promotes a peaceful political path, it continues to commemorate IRA actions, often claiming there was no alternative at the time.

The Troubles: A violent conflict in Northern Ireland from the late 1960s to 1998, resulting in over 3,500 deaths. The conflict largely pitted Catholic and Protestant communities against each other over political, religious, and identity issues. Paramilitary groups from both sides carried out bombings, assassinations, and violence, often affecting their own people. The Good Friday Agreement of 1998, supported by both communities, ended the conflict and laid the foundation for peace in Northern Ireland.

SECRETS OF THE RED CAPS

Copyright © Maurice Wylie Media, 2025

Paperback ISBN: 978-1-915223-49-4

eBook   ISBN: 978-1-915223-50-0

All rights reserved.

No part of this publication may be reproduced, stored in a retrieval system, or transmitted in any form or by any means, electronic, mechanical, photocopying or otherwise, without the prior written consent of the publisher, except as provided by United Kingdom copyright law. Short extracts may be used for review purposes

Every effort has been made to trace copyright holders and to obtain permission for the use of copyrighted material. The publisher apologises for any errors or omissions and would be grateful if notified of any corrections that should be incorporated in future reprints or editions of this book.

Published by

Maurice Wylie Media
Specialist in Life Stories

Based in Northern Ireland, distributing across the world.

Sgt Graham Chipperfield and his six-man section of RMP JNCOs in Clooney Base, Londonderry

Special Recognition

To Graham Chipperfield, whose courage in sharing his story made this book possible. His distinguished service includes roles as Corporal and Sergeant in the Royal Military Police (Regular), Captain in the Royal Military Police (Territorial Army), and Flight Lieutenant in the Royal Air Force. Graham continues to serve as Vice-Chairman of his Regimental Association in Northern Ireland.

Special thanks to our research team, whose additional insights into the locations and context of the Troubles have added depth and detail that further honours all who served, especially those who made the supreme sacrifice.

Contents

DEDICATION 5
GLOSSARY 9
INTRODUCTION 19

SECTION ONE
THE JOURNEY BEGINS

1. Mummy's Boy 25
2. Plastic Guns – Special Ops 29

SECTION TWO
NORTHERN IRELAND

3. The Straitjacket 39
4. Green as Grass 45
5. The Country Boils 51
6. Singing a Rebel Song 59
7. Captain Black & The UDA 65
8. Our First Red Cap Falls 71

9.	We Walked the Blocks	77
10.	"Rat Trap at Flak Jacket One – Over!"	97
11.	Death Comes Looking	101
12.	Arms Dump Uncovered	107
13.	Boys Will Be Boys	115
14.	The Dark World of Informing	119
15.	Upholding the Law	135
16.	Ten Years Later	143
17.	The British Ambassador - Not	159
18.	We Only Have to Be Lucky Once	165
19.	Time for Change	187

EPILOGUE	205

SECTION THREE

WEAPONS USED DURING OPERATION BANNER

BRITISH ARMY WEAPONS	211
TERRORIST WEAPONS	221

Introduction

The legacy of Northern Ireland's Troubles is not only written in politics and headlines – it lives on in the personal accounts of those who served, suffered, and survived. Yet too many of these stories remain hidden, unspoken, or deliberately forgotten.

Secrets of the Red Caps: Northern Ireland breaks that silence.

This book tells the powerful and often harrowing story of Sergeant Graham Chipperfield, a former Royal Military Police NCO whose journey through conflict, love and loss offers a rare, unfiltered glimpse into the human cost of military service during one of the most dangerous periods in British history. His story takes us to the front line – not only in terms of operations and covert missions – but of moral choices, personal sacrifices, and the emotional scars that linger still.

Graham's testimony carries particular weight. A close encounter with death in a bomb attack. A deeply personal relationship with a Northern Irish woman. A dramatic encounter with IRA commander Martin McGuinness. His account is both intensely personal and historically significant. Graham's honesty strikes you immediately, his courage becomes evident, and his memory proves precise.

The Truth Revealed Team worked alongside him in bringing this story to light. Through careful research, verification, and historical context, we helped place Sergeant Chipperfield's experience within the broader narrative of the Troubles, exposing realities often lost beneath political rhetoric or public silence.

This book does not seek to inflame old wounds or take sides. It forms part of a larger mission: to record truth whilst the people who lived it are still here to tell it. We believe that only through honest reflection can we honour those who suffered and ensure that future generations understand what peace actually costs.

The events in this book are rooted in documented experiences. Whilst presented through one man's eyes, they reflect the reality lived by many who served during the Troubles: the dangers faced, the decisions made under pressure, the consequences carried for decades.

We thank Graham Chipperfield for his courage in telling his story. We thank you, the reader, for being willing to face the truth, unvarnished and unrevised.

The Truth Revealed Team

Red Caps – The Name?

The Royal Military Police, or Red Caps, as we were nicknamed. In the early days, we wore the same colour of cap as other army officers. To distinguish us, a red elastic cloth would slip over the top of our caps – hence the name "Red Caps."

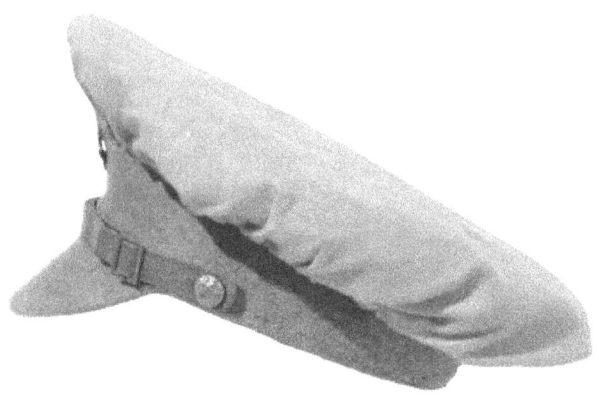

The Red Cap Cover

SECTION ONE

The Journey Begins

CHAPTER 1

Mummy's Boy

From the day I was born in Westhill Hospital, Dartford, England, on March 1, 1953, I did not have a great start in life. Mum, who had been medically discharged from the Royal Navy when she was a member of the Women's Royal Naval Service (WRNS) in 1951, was still convalescing from Tuberculosis and the birth was "difficult," causing me extensive facial bruising. If that was not bad enough, infantile eczema and asthma would cause me to spend a long time in Shooters Hill Hospital in South-East London. There is a small photograph in the family albums of me sitting in one of the old-fashioned cots in the hospital, with my hands in bandage gloves, to prevent me from scratching and injuring myself because of my eczema. Mum would have said that characterisation would set the tone for the rest of my life.

I, like many others, carry the utmost respect for my mother. Not only for those who gave birth, but those who worked their socks off to put food on the table as a one-parent family. That was my mum.

Even with Mum and me living with my grandparents in London, just to keep our overheads down, it was still difficult. My dad was serving with the Royal Military Police as part of the United Nations Forces in Korea.

Mum was employed as a conductress, or to give it its local name, a "Clippy" on London Transport trolley buses, and at Christmas, she took on extra work as a part-time local postwoman, just to buy me a simple present and ease the finances of my grandparents over the holidays.

I still remember the trolley buses as if it were yesterday. It was such a special time. They ran on electricity from overhead cables strung across streets and were extremely popular in the post-war years, before diesel became the method of motion. Occasionally, my mum would take me to work with her. Her usual route was from Bexleyheath Clock Tower to the Woolwich Arsenal and at other times she would have to travel further into central London. At those times, she would "stick a penny" into her cash bag and sit me just inside the passenger compartment and I felt on top of the world – a child who was loved, and innocent of mind, although that would change soon.

For reasons unknown, from a young age, I would try and damage myself. One day I got hold of a pair of metal knitting needles, sat down in front of an electric socket, and inserted the needles into it. Mum, it so happened, just caught sight of me as my arms started to twitch and jerk from the electricity surging through them. With her being at one side of the room and me at the other, like a flash of lightning, she had her arms around me and pulled me away from the wall.

On another occasion, Mum left me in the bath whilst she popped downstairs. She seemed to be away for a long time, and I became bored. And what do kids do when they are bored? They get up to mischief and I was no different. At the end of the bath, I found my grandfather's razor. I had watched him use it, so I knew what to do and began shaving my face and forehead. Now I don't wish to alarm you, but when my mum returned, I was sitting in a bath of pink water as the blood streamed down my body into it.

As if it was yesterday, I still remember January 1957 – it was one of the sunniest Januarys on record. Personally, I don't think I was the only child ever to do this, but there I was standing outside our home, with my eyes fixed on the sun; only to discover my eyes starting to hurt. You might be thinking why would this be significant? It would be a day that would impact my life more than just my eyes being hurt.

That evening a knock was heard at the front door of my grandmother's home; it would be a knock that would change my life … forever.

I was the first to hear it and being young and quick, I ran and opened the door with excitement. Standing on the doorstep was the biggest man I had ever seen. He was over six feet tall, wearing British Army khaki battledress, three white stripes on his arm, and a peaked hat that had a bright red top.

Then I heard the words, "Hello son, is your mum in?" Not knowing who he was but with him being dressed in an army uniform, I think I just stared with my mouth open until I heard, "Tell her Fred is here." Well, my young tongue was not used to the name "Fred" so turning towards the front room I announced, "Mum, Thread is at the door!"

There was a loud shrill squeal from my mum as she jumped off the seat and pushed me gently to one side while the man was ushered into the house with Mum doing her best to hug him, talk with him, and kiss him all at the same time. This man was 14481308 Sergeant Frederick William Chipperfield of the Corps of Royal Military Police (RMP), who had just got back from United Nations duties in Korea. This was the man I was to call "Dad" for the rest of his life. He knew of me, but I had never met him before.

Living with my mum and grandparents I had got used to using the name Phipps as my surname, as that was my mum's maiden name as well as my grandparent's name. One day my dad took me to the side and informed me that my name was not Phipps, but that maybe I was confusing it with the name of Phillip, Duke of Edinburgh who was of course married to HM The Queen. He then went on saying that my name was not right and that my name was actually Chipperfield. Dad then took a piece of paper and showed me how to write my name out. He explained to me that as I had been living with my Grandmother Phipps, I had thought that my surname was Phipps, but not Phillips. To a rising five-year-old, this made perfect sense.

Then my newly returned dad was posted to the Royal Military Police company in Colchester, Essex. On 6 February 1958, my brother Clifford was born in the military hospital on the garrison. In late 1958 Dad was promoted to Staff Sergeant and was posted to 227 Provost Company in Nicosia, Cyprus. My mum was on her own again, but this time with two little ones. Undeterred, all three of us made our way out to Cyprus via Southampton and the troopship *Devonshire*. Dad met us in Limassol, and we took up residence in a small village called Traconis, just outside Nicosia. On 3 December 1959, my mum gave birth to her third son and my second brother, Paul John, in the military hospital at Dhekelia on the south coast of Cyprus. It must have been a portent of things to come, because shortly afterwards Dad was posted to 3 Infantry Brigade Provost Company which was based in Dhekelia on the south coast, one of two Sovereign Base Areas owned by the British in Cyprus.

Whether I wanted it or not, we were now moving to a proper house, namely 6 Arakan Place. Little was I aware that this would be move number two out of what would become 38 moves during the rest of my life!

CHAPTER 2

Plastic Guns - Special Ops

I couldn't believe it when I discovered the house had two floors, with a real back garden that overlooked a valley, known locally as The Wadi, full of carob trees, ditches, small hills, and caves. Basically, the opposite of London. It was a natural playground for a young boy, and along with like-minded friends, I would stay out playing nearly all day, until called home.

One Christmas, all the boys in the neighbourhood received Airfix plastic replicas of the 7.62mm Self-Loading Rifle (SLR), which had recently replaced the .303 No 4 rifle. Sorry about the figures/details, but once a weapons trainer, always a weapons trainer. A little note for you: The SLR was much beloved by soldiers until it was replaced in 2000.

There must have been at least twenty of us all running around with these black plastic rifles playing "war." I didn't realise then, hiding from enemies with plastic weapons, that later in life I would be using that little boy's skill to stay alive on the streets of Belfast, Londonderry, and along the border of Northern Ireland.

For those of you who were never in the army or stationed on its grounds, let me share the luxury that is provided to those willing to sacrifice their lives to defend the innocent.

Dad got moved to 6 (Dog) Company and had the exclusive task of looking after and using dogs in police work. Our new home was in a place called Richmond Village. This was a village purely for the military, consisting of bungalows all painted pink. Imagine hard guys coming out of their front doors on a hot day with tattoos, muscles stretching their skin … dwelling in a pink house. No one would believe it!

My most distinct memories of our pink house were the cooking and electrical systems. The cooker was a solid black iron unit, oven and stove in one, fuelled by paraffin. The paraffin came in a large glass bottle, the kind you'd see on a water cooler, and it sat inverted in a holder at the back of the range. Once the fuel flowed, you'd strike a match to ignite it and begin cooking. Looking back, I'm not sure health and safety had even been invented yet.

The electrical system in the kitchen had a black box with a pull-down switch on the side. When switched "On" a bright red ruby glass indicator illuminated to let you know it was working. One night my dad asked me to go and switch the immersion heater on. As I pulled the switch, the whole box exploded, showering me with metal and glass. As they say in Northern Ireland, it scared the wits out of me. Mum gave Dad a real telling off, because unknown to me, you were not meant to have all the house lights on *and* the immersion heater at the same time. It overloaded the system. Similarly, one evening I was walking through the living room going to my bedroom when there was a terrific smash behind me. One of the glass globes enclosing the ceiling light had become detached and crashed to the floor just as I passed. I was beginning to think perhaps they were trying to get rid of me.

I don't mind paying rent, but when other "things" are in the house and are not helping to pay the rent, I do have a problem.

One morning my mum reported that she had been awoken by a scratching sound. Whilst checking around the rooms of our home, a mouse happened to pop its head out of a newly chewed hole, in her bedroom wall. Fearing that the mouse might cause mayhem through the night, Mum stuffed the hole with one of my dad's thick socks, making the mouse run back through the plasterboard wall. Washing her hands and looking like she had achieved what she had set out to do, Mum then got back into bed and closed her eyes. To this day she never knew why, but she opened one eye a couple of hours later, and lo and behold, the mouse had pushed the sock out of the hole and was playing with it on the carpet. The following morning, the pest controller was called.

You can see that when it came to accommodation, the Army never had luxury at the top of its list.

All good things have to come to an end. I had arrived in Cyprus as a spotty five-year-old with National Health spectacles, asthma, frequent colds and coughs. At nine I was a healthy boy who could swim, snorkel, dive in seawater, play football on a pitch without a blade of grass on it, and camp out with the Cub Scouts in a eucalyptus plantation, without the need for mosquito repellent.

In 1963 Dad was posted to the Royal Military Police Training Centre in Woking, Surrey. I went to the local primary school when I was just ten. We spent just over a year there and in 1964, the entire training centre moved to Chichester in Sussex. This was a place I was to become well acquainted with in the future. It was from Chichester that in September 1964 I set out to attend the Duke of York's Royal Military School (DOYRMS) in Dover. I was to remain at the school until 1970, by which time Dad had moved to Berlin, then to Aldershot and then Hong Kong. (The latter was the best posting of all, as I first went there for a Christmas holiday in 1968, and in total, before he returned to the UK, I visited him four times.)

In the first week of July 1970, we were all back in England, as Dad was assigned as the Permanent Staff Officer (PSO) to a TA Training Centre in Millbrook Road, Southampton. The first and only bit of career advice I ever received from him was on receipt of my school examination results letter, when my dad exclaimed, "Well, it's down to the Army Careers Information Office (ACIO) for you on Monday." For Dad, the Army was the answer to everything.

That Monday came and Dad and I went to the Army Careers Information Office. After an interview with a genuinely nice, retired Lieutenant Colonel, it was decided that I should attend the Regular Commissions Board (RCB) at Westbury in Wiltshire, to see if I had any potential officer qualities. The minimum requirement was five "O" Levels, including Maths and English, and I was deficient in Maths.

At the opportune time I mentioned this to the Lieutenant Colonel, at which point he stated, "Seeing as you are a Dukie,[1] you're half-trained. Let us see how you get on." Eventually, a letter arrived inviting me to Westbury, the Army Officer Selection Board assessment centre. Unfortunately, I had decided to develop a stinking cough and cold, so I was feeling slightly under the weather when I turned up.

I had two days of intense testing, and I thought I did all right. Being the youngest in my group – I was just seventeen and a half – I felt very intimidated. Even during group discussions, I was so nervous that I only said two words over the whole session. We then had to take part in a Planning and Appreciation exercise. It took me far too long, and it was not until the debrief that I realised I had mucked it up. The plan itself was good, and I fought my corner against a very loud bloke from Newcastle who had a plan that he was determined to impose upon the group.

My cold and cough greatly affected my ability to breathe and get around the course. I managed just over one circuit whereas everyone else managed two. I did very well in the Command Task, getting my task done in quick time. However, overall, I did not expect to pass, and it was no surprise when a confirming letter arrived at home.

---

[1] "Dukies" refers to the students and alumni of The Duke of York"s Royal Military School (DOYRMS), a co-educational academy with a military tradition.

Chapter 2 - Plastic Guns - Special Ops

Even with failure, there came hope. The Board stated that I had "something to offer" and suggested that I go back to college, get the needed "O" Level and perhaps an "A" Level and present myself again in a year's time. In reality, I was awarded a "Deferred Watch." Meaning, they recognised something in me, but wanted me to get an "A" Level, or two if I could, and return. So not a total pass nor a total failure either.

Unfortunately, my dad did not see it that way and made it clear that he would not support me any further in my education, reminding me, "You had your chance," and informing me that joining up was my only alternative. So back we went to the Army Careers Information Office and Dad persuaded me to join the Royal Corps of Signals because, as he said, "You need a trade." I took the oath and the Queen's shilling and signed on the dotted line.

Eventually, the invitation to join the Army arrived, and I went and made my Attestation promise at the Army Careers Information Office. There, I was issued with a train warrant to get me to Catterick, and once my suitcase was packed, I was off. The date was October 10, 1970; the same time period when Northern Ireland was starting to collapse into a bloodbath. In the meantime, I was off to Catterick and 11 Signals Regiment to do my Basic Training.

The first obstacle to get over was to "Pass off the Square," which meant you had to demonstrate that you could march, halt, salute, about turn, march away and keep to your dressing and static foot drill.

Until then, our berets did not have cap badges on them, as we were considered too lowly to have such an honour. We had to march everywhere, and one day I was on my own marching back from the Quartermaster's Stores, when I saw an officer approaching. We had been instructed not to salute as we had no cap badge, but years of being at a military school took over, and I demonstrated the smartest eyes left, and salute on the march I can ever remember doing. I was immediately told to halt by the officer, who asked me my name and why I had saluted. I explained that it was a natural reaction, having been to military school. He told me to carry on. That evening, I was summoned to the troop commander's office and told to put my cap badge onto my beret immediately and spend the next morning looking at the clock whilst the others passed off the square!

I was awarded a "silver" matchbox cover with a "Jimmy" (emblem of the Royal Signals, a figure of a winged Mercury) on it for "Best Recruit Rifle Shot." I kept it for years, but I have no idea where it is now. I managed to obtain five "O" Levels, including Maths, whilst in the Royal Signals and after Basic Training was moved into the Potential Officer squadron as I had the required background and educational qualifications. Sometime later, it was decided that perhaps my future would be better served as a junior signalman with a Trade. I was offered Trade Training in whatever trade I wished. I chose to become a Specialist Operator (Spec Op).

Spec Ops

Spec Ops involved radio operators who, once trained, sat at a receiver with headphones on and a typewriter in front of them. They were assigned a frequency to monitor, and whatever came through in Morse code, they had to type down. This was GCHQ-type radio interception but at a very basic level. To gain the knowledge to understand Morse code and typing, the working week was divided into teaching periods. The only subjects were Morse, Typing, Electricity and Circuit Training, filling eight lessons or training periods a day. That was it! For nine months, that was the total number of subjects you had to study.

There were only three places in the world where these operators could be posted: Winchester, Germany, or Cyprus.

Typing lessons began with a set of headphones and a typewriter. The instructor then switched on a tape recorder and some very stilted music consisting of a piano and drum started playing a rhythm that you were meant to hit the typewriter keyboard to. Starting with the left hand on the top line of QWERTYUIOP: QWE, space bar; right hand, RTY, space bar; then UIO, space bar; and finally, PPP! The letters alternated left and right. You typed at a speed that was known as "two words a fortnight." It was brain-numbing. Similarly, for Morse training, we had the same headsets but this time a series of "dots" and "dashes" was transmitted to us. The speed was dead slow to start with, and we had to quickly learn the difference between P (di-dah-dit) and X (dah-di-dah). Well, this was all extremely exciting – not!

In the Mess Hall, blokes were tapping out Morse code messages to each other with their knives and forks. The Regimental Sergeant Major (RSM) saw me struggling and told me, "When you're in town, you should read billboard adverts and convert them into Morse code." Code for – you're not too good at this.

It took me just a week to realise this was not for me and to ask that I be released and allowed to return to civilian life. But there was just one problem. According to the staff in the administration office, I had signed on for nine years. This was news to me, because under the terms of joining as a Potential Officer, I was given an "S-type" engagement that meant the Army, or I, could end our contract whenever we wanted to. There was no commitment by either party due to the uncertainty of officer training. However, it appeared that in leaving Catterick and signing many papers, I had signed a paper committing me to nine years of service. I was completely unaware of this and concluded that someone had slipped the paper in without my knowledge. I was told to go away and come back in the afternoon. The RSM sent for me and informed me that I was, "in for nine years." I explained that I had no knowledge of this, and if he persisted, I would have no alternative but to telephone my dad – by now Captain

Fred Chipperfield of the Royal Military Police serving in Northern Ireland – and tell him what had happened. I was told to wait outside the office. Twenty minutes later, I was issued a rail ticket and told to make my way back to Catterick to be discharged!

SECTION TWO

Northern Ireland

CHAPTER 3

The Straitjacket

When Split Seconds Mean Life or Death

When British troops first arrived in Northern Ireland in 1969, they weren't just welcomed by the Catholic population with tea and buns – they genuinely wondered what all the fuss was about. Lads found themselves chatting with locals, accepting cups of tea from grateful residents, wondering why they'd been sent to what looked like any other British town. Reality hit hard later on. Misguided government initiatives, followed by heavy-handed military responses, lit the fuse for the real Troubles. Before long, the very people we had been sent to protect, the Catholics, were the ones joining the IRA to kill us.

What started as peacekeeping turned into something none of us had bargained for.

No Clear Orders

One of the biggest problems at the start of military involvement in Northern Ireland was the complete lack of clear directions on what troops should, or could, do. Legally speaking, the situation was unlike anything in modern British military history. These weren't enemy fighters on some foreign battlefield – these were citizens on United Kingdom soil, and some of them were actively trying to kill British soldiers.

You'd think if someone started shooting at you, you would simply shoot back. Basic self-defence, right? But it wasn't that simple. What if you spotted someone with a weapon? What if you'd just watched a mate get shot by a gunman who then vanished into a crowd? Could you open fire? At whom? When?

These weren't theoretical debates for a lecture hall. These were life-and-death decisions that eighteen and nineteen-year-old lads had to make in seconds, often in the dark, usually under fire, with adrenaline pumping and their mate's lives on the line.

The Yellow Card – Straitjacket

The military's answer to all this was the Yellow Card – a small document meant to give guidance to troops in Northern Ireland. Every soldier had to carry one and know exactly what it allowed – and forbade – them to do.

Just three pages of text that were supposed to govern when you could use lethal force. Those three pages could mean the difference between a lawful action and a court-martial, between going home to your family and spending years in prison.

Even a single page showed how complicated the decisions were. According to the card, you were entitled to shoot someone about to throw a petrol bomb. Fair enough – a petrol bomb could kill or seriously injure soldiers or civilians. But the card didn't say you *had* to shoot. That was the problem many soldiers faced: the final decision to open fire was entirely theirs.

Making The Decision

Picture this: you're nineteen, standing on a Belfast street corner at two in the morning. A crowd is gathering, tension is building, and suddenly someone lights what looks like a petrol bomb. You've got maybe three seconds to decide. Is it really a petrol bomb? Is he going to throw it? Are civilians close enough to be hit if you fire? Can you stop him without killing him?

The Yellow Card – or, as I liked to call it, *The Straitjacket* – offered guidance, but it couldn't decide for you. Its rules were clear enough: fire only as a last resort, only at identified targets, only with aimed single shots. No spraying bullets into crowds. No firing without a visible target. And every shot would be justified and investigated afterwards.

The pressure was enormous. Fire too quickly and you might kill an innocent person – face a murder charge, ruin your life, and shame your unit. Wait too long and your mate next to you might be the one burning to death from a petrol bomb you could have stopped.

Vehicle Checkpoints

Vehicle checkpoints were particularly tricky. The card said you *may* open fire on a vehicle if it's deliberately driven at someone and there's no other way to stop it. But that didn't mean every car that crashed through a checkpoint was fair game. Had it actually hit anybody? Was it aimed at a soldier on purpose? Or was it just some terrified driver who panicked and hit the accelerator instead of the brake?

These distinctions might sound academic, but they marked the line between justified shooting and criminal action. Investigators would examine everything afterwards: the car's speed and direction, whether the driver seemed to be aiming, whether you'd given warnings, and what alternatives existed. A soldier's career – and freedom – often depended on split-second judgements made under extreme stress.

The Full Aide Memoire

The Yellow Card was just part of it. The complete Aide Memoire was like a small book, about the size of a five-year diary. Over fifteen sections covering everything you might face in Northern Ireland. First aid procedures next to guidance on military dogs. Arrest procedures alongside what to do if you accidentally crossed into the Republic – a potentially explosive diplomatic cock-up.

Each section existed because of lessons learned, often through bitter experience. The border crossing rules were there because soldiers had wandered across unmarked boundaries before and created international incidents. The detailed arrest procedures were there because botched arrests meant terrorist suspects walking free on technicalities.

Living With It

For us carrying these cards, they were both protection and burden. Follow the rules and you have legal backing. Step outside them, even under pressure, and you could face criminal charges. The card was supposed to be your legal shield, but it felt more like a straitjacket when the shooting started.

Many lads spent time studying these pages by torchlight in their bunks, memorising the exact words, trying to imagine how they'd apply the rules when everything went mad. Because when the moment came – and it always did eventually – there'd be no time to check the card, no chance for a committee decision. Just you, your training, your judgement, and knowing that whatever you decided in those few seconds would follow you for the rest of your life.

The Yellow Card was meant to make things clearer in an impossible situation. What it actually did was put the terrible responsibility squarely on every soldier's shoulders: knowing that the next decision you made might be the most important – and most examined – of your entire life.

Chapter 3 - The Straitjacket 43

RESTRICTED

INSTRUCTIONS FOR OPENING FIRE IN NORTHERN IRELAND

General Rules

1. In all situations you are to use the minimum force necessary. FIREARMS MUST ONLY BE USED AS A LAST RESORT.
2. Your weapon must always be made safe: that is, NO live round is to be carried in the breech and in the case of automatic weapons the working parts are to be forward, unless you are ordered to carry a live round in the breech or you are about to fire.

Challenging

3. A challenge MUST be given before opening fire unless:
    a. to do so would increase the risk of death or grave injury to you or any other person;
    b. you or others in the immediate vicinity are being engaged by terrorists.
4. You are to challenge by shouting "ARMY: STOP OR I FIRE" or words to that effect.

Opening Fire

5. You may only open fire against a person:
    a. if he* is committing or about to commit an act LIKELY TO ENDANGER LIFE, AND THERE IS NO OTHER WAY TO PREVENT THE DANGER. The following are some examples of acts where life could be endangered, dependent always upon the circumstances.
        (i) firing or being about to fire a weapon;
        (ii) planting, detonating or throwing an explosive device (including a petrol bomb);
        (iii) deliberately driving a vehicle at a person and there is no other way of stopping him*;
    b. if you know that he* has just killed or injured any person by such means and he* does not surrender if challenged, and THERE IS NO OTHER WAY TO MAKE AN ARREST.
6. If you have to open fire you should:
    a. fire only aimed shots;
    b. fire no more rounds than are necessary;
    c. take all reasonable precautions not to injure anyone other than your target.

* 'She can be read instead of 'he' if applicable.

RESTRICTED 11—1 /3

YELLOW CARD

The above is an example of the famous – or infamous – Yellow Card, which was meant to give guidance to the troops involved in Northern Ireland. By order, we all had to carry a copy of this and fully understand what it allowed us to do. Please look at the example above, which is only one page of three. You will note that according to these orders, one was entitled to shoot at someone about to throw a petrol bomb.

Of course, it does not say you *must* shoot. That was the dilemma that many soldiers faced because finally, it was your decision and your decision only to open fire. The Yellow Card did not give *carte blanche* to just fire into a crowd. Identified targets, only fire as a last resort and only aimed single shots. It also states that you *may* open fire on a vehicle if it is deliberately driven at a person and there is no other way of stopping it. This does not mean you can open fire on a vehicle that has crashed through a Vehicle Checkpoint (VCP) if it has not injured someone or been deliberately aimed at someone.

CHAPTER 4

Green as Grass

1972 is remembered as the bloodiest year of the Troubles in Northern Ireland: 479 people were slain, including 130 British soldiers, and 4,876 were injured. The violence peaked with events like *Bloody Sunday* in Derry/Londonderry, where British paratroopers returned fire at the IRA who used innocent civilians as human shields, killing 13 unarmed civil rights protesters. Then there was *Bloody Friday* in Belfast, where the IRA detonated 22 bombs in just over an hour, killing nine people and injuring 130 others. Yet, amid the carnage, life went on. Alex Higgins claimed the World Professional Snooker Championship, Mary Peters became the first woman from Northern Ireland to win an Olympic gold in Munich, where terrorists brutally murdered 11 Israeli athletes.

The following year, in 1973, The Sunningdale Agreement was signed by British Prime Minister Edward Heath,[2] Taoiseach Liam Cosgrave,[3] Brian Faulkner,[4] Gerry Fitt[5] and Oliver Napier,[6] which left the country on a trigger edge.

---

[2] Sir Edward Heath was Prime Minister during a time of industrial upheaval and economic decline, in which he led Britain into the European Community.

[3] As the Taoiseach of the Republic of Ireland, Cosgrave is perhaps best known for his strong stance against terrorism and political violence during the Troubles.

[4] Brian Faulkner, the leader of the UUP, was the sixth and last Prime Minister of Northern Ireland.

[5] Gerry Fitt, the leader of the SDLP, was never backward in criticising the IRA and was dedicated to non-violence, justice, and equality.

[6] Sir Oliver Napier was a solicitor and co-founder of the Alliance Party. In 1985 he was knighted in the Queen"s Birthday Honours. It was a bold decision for someone from a Catholic background during the height of the Troubles.

I rejoined the Army and specifically the Royal Military Police (RMP) in October 1971. The following month, I arrived at Chichester's Royal Military Police Training Centre (RMPTC, or affectionately "Depot") to begin my training. I remained there until January 1972. After a short delay to represent the Army at under-19 rugby, I was posted as a newly promoted Lance Corporal (LCpl) to 247 (Berlin) Provost Company (Pro Coy). In March 1972, I started a two-year stint learning the trade of a Junior Non-Commissioned Officer (JNCO), playing a lot of rugby, getting into minor trouble with Army discipline, having a great time in Germany's capital, and finally meeting an English girl whom I decided to marry.

In March 1974, between postings from Berlin to Northern Ireland, I had just been married in Lyme Regis on 2 March to Alison Elizabeth Emmett, and I was exactly 21 years and 19 days old. I was driving to Liverpool to catch the sailing to Belfast for my next posting. Booking into the local hotel, I was given a room that was very grim and grotty. Throughout the night, it became apparent that I was not in bed by myself; something was already at home and sharing the bed with me. Exhausted from the drive, I fell asleep, determined in the morning to find out more.

The morning couldn't come early enough. I don't know why, but I lay scratching, looking at the clock, waiting for the alarm to go off, then I got up and when I looked in the mirror, I was covered in bites. I quickly washed and dressed. It was time to go as I said *goodbye* to a room and hotel that I would never return to.

Arriving in Belfast in the morning, my dad was waiting on the quayside in his car to escort me to Alexander Barracks.

My dad and I shared many common interests, so I was excited to see him. However, I realised something was not right when the normal welcome smile was gone. As he hugged me and said, "Follow me!" I was astounded. There was no waiting around or "how are you"; I knew something was wrong.

Chapter 4 - Green as Grass

Dad was already serving in Northern Ireland and had been since 1972; he was a Major[7] and the quartermaster[8] of Alexander Barracks, which housed the HQs of both 1st and 2nd Regiments of the Royal Military Police along with 3 Provost Companies and a Company of Women's Royal Army Corps Provost. The barracks had been built alongside the RAF Aldergrove Station which itself shared the airfield facilities with Belfast Airport (later to become Belfast International Airport).

Dad jumped into his car, I into mine, and off he went with me on his tail. As I drove, I pondered, "Are there no main roads in Northern Ireland? Why are we speeding, then slowing down, then speeding and taking chances at road junctions? At this rate, the police will be pulling us over."

As this was before there was GPS and many of the road signs were missing, it was imperative for me not to lose Dad on these numerous corners, turns and so forth. The 45-minute drive felt like two hours as Dad finally drew up at the entrance of the barracks. The guards requested ID from him, even though they knew him – this was protocol. Enough said. He drove through the main entrance and waited for me to come through security. I did think he would have told the guards that his son was behind him, but the way they looked at me, asking me to get out of the car, open the boot and so forth, I wondered…

In all the times I had driven into a barracks in England, I never had to go through so much checking, but here in Northern Ireland, this was on another level.

As soon as Dad saw me coming through the entrance, he drove off and I followed, his driving now changed to something more normal.

---

[7] A major will command a sub-unit, typically around 120 officers and soldiers. They are responsible for their training, welfare, and administration both in barracks and on operations, as well as the management of their equipment.

[8] A quartermaster is responsible for ensuring that the soldiers and units have the equipment, materials, and systems needed for missions.

He pulled up outside the barrack blocks and company offices of 175 Provost Company Royal Military Police and signalled me to follow him. Collecting any personal items from my car boot, I followed him as he led me into the building. As soon as he found a private space, he turned and looked me in the eyes and said in his military tone… "What the hell were you thinking of?"

Startled by what was taking place, I don't think I even said anything when he repeated, "What the hell were you doing driving that car in Northern Ireland?"

It was then that it hit me.

From the end of WWII until the Troubles, all military personnel stationed in Germany had distinctive number plates, which were white with black lettering. Because of this, spotting a vehicle owned or driven by a military person or a family member was easy.

There was the outrageous murder of an airman, his wife, and his child in Holland as they had stopped in a car park and the IRA spotted the number plates and gunned them all to death.

The officer murdered in Bielefeld was the same. They just followed his distinctive number-plated car to his home.

Once the Government/MOD woke up, they immediately instituted a new system whereby UK-style number plates, i.e. black on yellow, white on black, were allotted to the BFG Licensing Office in Germany and issued to military personnel. It caused some bother as genuine UK tourists in Germany could be pulled over by the Military Police, if they were in a military garrison, for a spot check. Likewise, some newly plated BFG vehicles driving in the UK did not show up when a plate check was done by the UK police, leading to some arrests for having false registrations. Eventually, late in 2014, after people including myself

Chapter 4 - Green as Grass

suggested that the BFG Office issue its own plates – the same design as those in the UK but part of a batch of numbers given by DVLA Swansea to the military authorities in Germany – the system was adopted *in toto*. Just as an addition, all left-hand drive cars owned by military personnel were given German-style number plates, as were motorcycles. It would not have taken the IRA too much brain power to work out that a left-hand drive vehicle with UK plates in a garrison area was more than likely driven by a soldier.

No matter that I had just been promoted to Corporal in the Corps of Royal Military Police before leaving Germany, here was I coming off the boat in Belfast, driving my British Forces Germany (BFG) registered car, as I did not know how or have the time to get my car UK registered, and really advertising to the IRA, "Hi guys I'm over here!" My father's reaction was a wake-up call – I was as green as grass,[9] unprepared, and lucky still to be standing there at all.

---

[9] Someone is completely inexperienced or naive.

CHAPTER 5

The Country Boils

After the straight talking from Dad, and a handshake – Dad never hugged – he walked away saying, "Take care of yourself." Although that was his way of showing he loved me, I believe that when he said it, it carried a whole different meaning than when he said it back in England.

I was now walking to my barracks when the Company Sergeant Major (CSM)[10] and the Officer Commanding (OC)[11] met me. The first thing I received from them was a good bollocking. I had arrived without shaving! I stood there with my poker face on, knowing I couldn't show what I was feeling inside. I thought that it was a bit harsh, since I hadn't even had time to go to the restroom, let alone shave. I knew that they would never be interested in the "whys."

I was introduced to my Platoon Commander[12] and the rest of the lads of No 1 Platoon and assigned a bed space in the barrack block, as there were no married quarters available. In my barracks room, there were four of us. The three who were already there had made themselves comfortable as much as they could, as the room was just for sleeping in.

---

[10] A CSM in the British Army is responsible for maintaining discipline, ensuring soldiers behave in line with Army standards, and advising the company commander on soldier-related matters.

[11] An OC in the British Army is responsible for commanding a sub-unit or minor unit, such as a company or squadron.

[12] A Platoon Commander in the British Army is responsible for leading and training a platoon of soldiers on exercises and operations.g and training a platoon of soldiers on exercises and operations.

Otherwise, we would be out on patrol. Each "bedspace" comprised a single bed, a tall locker in which to hang clothes and a "soldier box." This was a wooden chest which could be secured with a padlock and into which you placed all your valuable items. As I was only going to be in the barracks room for a short time, I did not unpack everything. The three lads in the room had been in Northern Ireland for some time and knew a lot about the place. They had a record player and to my astonishment, would play 45rpm singles bought from a record shop that sold Republican or "Rebel" music. I distinctly remember "We are on the one road, sharing the one load" and "The Ballad of Joe McCann" along with a song about the internment prison at Long Kesh. One lad named John had a large poster on the wall next to his bed showing some serious attitude: basically, "F" the world. It seemed to sum up how everyone in the platoon felt. Even as I write this, the hairs on my arms still rise when I think back to that time.

The Ulster Workers Council[13] had called a General Strike because they did not want to share power in the Stormont Parliament with Republicans. Loyalists had erected barricades across the country - makeshift checkpoints where drivers were stopped and questioned, and roads were forcibly closed. The atmosphere was volatile, or as the saying goes, *"the kettle is boiling."* In other words, pressure was building to a dangerous level, and if the kettle wasn't lifted off the heat soon – if tensions weren't defused – it was only a matter of time before something exploded.

---

[13] "The Ulster Workers Council" was a loyalist workers organisation set up in Northern Ireland in 1974.

Chapter 5 - The Country Boils

Tens of thousands attend a rally at Stormont

The following day I entered the briefing room and listened intently to the Sergeant on the plan for that day, including which areas (if any) we had to stay out of.

Unaware of what to expect when I left the barracks on my first patrol, I was shown how to draw a weapon from the armoury, sign for it, load it with live rounds, and put a flak jacket on: no easy feat. I was then shown how to sit in the back of a Land Rover. I wasn't sure if all the learning was out of "love for this boy" or just treating me like a child – time would tell.

There was little – if any – conversation between us, because the noise from the open rear doors of the Land Rover was too much as we rolled into Lisburn. It remained quiet, and around midnight we drove into the local barracks – Thiepval Barracks – and slept in a small room until morning, when we got up and drove back to Aldergrove.

I had little knowledge of Northern Ireland or its problems, apart from a bit of studying for my "O" Level History examination. I remember one phrase that our history master, Mr Jack Clarke – known as Jack Razz, an old queen who, if he were around today, would be jailed for his abuse of young boys – used to quote: "The Irish are always revolting, in many ways. They do not know what they want, but they will fight anyone to get it."

Two examples of not being prepared for Northern Ireland stick in my mind from those early days in Belfast. I cannot recall the actual rotation of our duties, but one afternoon, with the RUC being busy, the patrol I was in was told to go to a bar on Castlereagh Street near the Short Strand, where there was a disturbance.

On arrival, there were two elderly people, one male and one female, on the pavement, both drunk, shouting and swearing at each other in a Belfast dialect...

"Catch yerself on, ye auld Irish eejit," the woman shouted.

"Look who's talkin', ye clatterin' oul bat," the man fired back.

Next thing, a black taxi screeched up, she jumped in, and off she went like a fart in the wind.

I turned to my mate and said, "I don't get it… aren't they both Irish?"

He just shook his head, saying, "Sweet sufferin' Jaysus, Chippy! You've some amount of learnin' to do."

A few days later, I was told to go to an address just off the Shankill Road, accompanied by a Staff Sergeant (SSgt) who had been a Sergeant Instructor at the Royal Military Police Training Centre when I was a recruit. He had arrived on the same boat as me from the mainland, and consequently knew about as much as I did. The driver was a Corporal with far more experience than we had.

When we arrived, we found a foot patrol from the Parachute Regiment inside and outside the terraced house.

They explained that they had raided the place and found a gas cylinder bomb under the stairs, a pistol down the back of a sofa, and several plastic bags with "interesting" items inside. My SSgt turned to me and ordered me to start loading the stuff into our vehicle. For evidential purposes, the items found by the Paras were treated as an "explosive or arms find" and had to be handed over to the RUC. As the intermediary between the soldiers on the ground and the RUC, it was our job to secure and process the evidence for onward transmission and handling.

The Bomb Disposal Officer, or Ammunition Technical Officer (ATO),[14] then arrived and having examined the gas cylinder bomb, arranged for the owner of the house, the bomb maker, to be brought to the scene. When he arrived the Ammunition Technical Officer told him, "I can blow the bomb up in your house, or you can move it."

I couldn't believe what I was about to see. The bloke walked over, picked up the bomb and was directed down the street towards a building site.

"You go with him to make sure he doesn't escape," said the SSgt to me, "and one of the Paras will go along as well." And off we went, the three of us.

The Para began teasing the bomber with the SLR[15] pointing at his head, "Go on mate, make a run for it, I won't shoot you." Glad to say he didn't run.

---

[14] Ammunition Technical Officers (ATOs) in the British Army are experts in ammunition, explosives, weapons intelligence, and bomb disposal.

[15] The L1A1 Self-Loading Rifle (SLR) was the primary weapon used by British soldiers in Northern Ireland during the 1970s and later in the Falklands war.

The Para was told where to go by the bomb maker. My picture subsequently appeared in the Daily Mail, showing me escorting the bomb maker down the street.

Graham, escorting the bombmaker

Newspaper Extract - Man with the cannister of death

Guarded by troops, a terrorist walks carefully along a Belfast street carrying his own bomb.

The man carried the 30lb of explosives packed into a gas cylinder, hugged to his chest, for 150 yards to a patch of waste ground.

The drama began when men of the 3rd Parachute Regiment raided a terrorist house in the Protestant Shankill Road area and found a bomb-making factory upstairs.

At first the Army disposal expert decided he would have to explode the bomb where it stood, inevitably damaging many homes nearby.

Then the man arrested inside the house volunteered to carry it to open ground where it would be blown up safely. He was followed on the walk by an officer with his rifle trained at his back.

At the end of the street was a building site and the terrorist carried the bomb into the site and placed it on a pile of sand, where it was partly covered before being detonated in situ by the Ammunition Technical Officer. Once the bomb was made safe, we invited the Ammunition Technical Officer to look at the stuff in our Land Rover. I was standing at the back of it looking in, and the SSgt was sitting on the tailboard fiddling with something that looked like a screwdriver. Just then, there was a loud bang. I felt myself being grabbed by a large Para and dragged into a doorway. "You get in here son," he said. From the back of my Land Rover, I could hear the SSgt laughing. He had accidentally fired a "Zip" gun, which was in fact a small homemade weapon that looked like a screwdriver and fired a .22 bullet. Small but deadly, the bullet had passed between my feet and ricocheted away down the street.

The Ammunition Technical Officer then started looking at the stuff in the back. "These bags are full of ANFO (Ammonium Nitrate and Fuel Oil, the homemade explosive mixture favoured by both sides). Get them out of your truck," he told us.

Inside a Wellington boot, he found a primed and ready nail bomb. Finally, what we had thought was a washing line was Cortex, a detonating cord used to initiate an explosion. Explosive material in a washing line-like coil. "Bloody hell," said the Ammunition Technical Officer, "you lot trying to kill yourselves?" So much for arriving straight off the boat into the conflict of Northern Ireland. It was a lot different the second time around, but more of that later.

I was either at Castlereagh RUC Station and patrolling East Belfast or at Ardmillan House, an old Dr Barnardo's Home, in Fortwilliam Park in West Belfast. The latter duty consisted of waiting until called to go to any of the many military HQs of the regiments and corps based in Belfast and collect either weapons, ammunition, or people that had been seized or arrested by the security forces.

For example, if the soldiers based at Grand Central Hotel (GCH) in the heart of Belfast arrested someone, we would collect them from Grand Central Hotel and depending on which part of the city they were arrested in, we would take them to either Queen Street, North Queen Street, Musgrave Street, Hastings Street or Old Park RUC Station.

We would then proceed to the RUC Station covering that area and hand over the items or people to the RUC. This was to maintain continuity of evidence, should the find or arrest result in a court case. This meant that we had to have extensive knowledge of the locations of all the RUC stations in Belfast, and there were quite a few, and how to get into and out of them via safe routes.

The further out one went from the city centre, it could mean delivering items to Andersonstown, Springfield Road or Tennant Street RUC Station. As Catholic and hence Nationalist or Republican people occupied West Belfast, most of our work involved West Belfast and its RUC Stations. To avoid military vehicles from various Army units dashing about all over Belfast, the task fell to us to collect and deliver.

I was in 175 Pro Coy, Royal Military Police, nicknamed "The Heavies" as we were mounted in Long Wheel Base Land Rovers that were covered with Makralon, a so-called bulletproof armour.

The first day I went on the ranges to fire my weapons in training, the Platoon Commander placed a plate of Makralon at the end of the 25-metre range. He then put five or six 9mm bullets straight through it. "It might protect you from bricks, stones and petrol bombs," he said, "but it isn't bulletproof." I thought, "Is anyone getting paid to *think* here?"

CHAPTER 6

Singing a Rebel Song

Our patrol base in West Belfast was housed in an ex-Barnardo's Home called Ardmillan House. It stood just off the Antrim Road, in Fortwilliam Park.

Ardmillian House, as it was when the Company moved in

When on patrol, my job was to ride "shotgun." I was to sit in the back of the Land Rover and provide cover for the vehicle from the rear. There would have been just the three of us in the Land Rover: the senior man or vehicle commander was in the front passenger seat with the driver next to him. I would sit alone in the back.

I still remember those first few times of going on patrol in the Land Rover. I would climb into the back, and as we left the compound, I would cock my Sterling 9mm SMG in readiness to open fire. My adrenaline was flowing - waiting to hear a crack of a bullet hitting us or the order "Out!" It turned out all quiet for another night.

This night when I returned to our base, as was routine, I took the magazine off my SMG, cleared it and secured it in the armoury, when the Platoon Commander, a Staff Sergeant, spotted me and called me into his office.

I stood there in front of his desk, not sure why I had been called in, then the Staff Sergeant asked, "Anything wrong with your SMG?"

"No Staff," I replied.

"Well, I hear that it keeps cocking itself when you leave here."

Unknown to me, the two colleagues who were on my patrol had reported me, as a cocked weapon behind their backs was making them a bit nervous. So, when the SSgt had framed the question, that was his way of saying it was dangerous.

He did not need to say anything else – I had got the message loud and clear – and I stopped doing what was an incorrect and plainly dangerous drill.

We were trained to react quickly and that came with risk, because when we were inside a "secure" location, we could place our unloaded weapons on our beds. I would lay my SMG on my bed and when an order came through, we would grab our weapons and race outside into the back of the Land Rover. As we would be running, we would be slipping a full magazine into the SMG, but that only happened when we had checked to ensure that the safety catch was on.

Chapter 6 - Singing a Rebel Song

On return to the barracks, we would be ordered to unload our weapons. This entailed pointing the SMG into a sandbagged bunker, checking the safety catch was on, and then removing the magazine. To be doubly safe, you were then required to take the safety catch off and work the bolt once or twice, just to make sure there was nothing "up the spout." As I did this, the bolt and the working parts of my SMG just slid backwards and forwards under no pressure at all. The bolt usually went forward under the pressure of a large spring in the body of the weapon. I quickly stripped the weapon down and found that someone had removed the spring! Obviously, this was to teach me not to cock my weapon when we went out, but in doing so...if we had come under fire, my weapon would not have functioned…

The result of this thoughtless prank was that for years afterwards, and in fact from time to time even now, I have nightmares where I am under fire, but my weapon won't function and I am up to my knees in 9mm bullets, but I cannot get any of them into a magazine to start shooting back. I tried not to think too much about it, but others I have discussed it with tell me I could be suffering from Post-Traumatic Stress Disorder (PTSD), even after all this time. It just proves that old saying, "One man's joke is another man's abuse."

Very late one night we had to go to an Army base in Roden Street in the Lower Falls and collect a prisoner. He was to be taken to Andersonstown RUC station and handed over. Because we were in a Land Rover and as explained, not exactly bulletproof, we were offered transport in a 1-ton Humber Armoured Car, known affectionately as a "Pig." With two prisoners, the arresting soldier and the three of us MPs, we started up the road towards Andersonstown. As we began the journey the two prisoners started to sing rebel songs at the top of their voices.

The soldier with us was upset at this and told them to shut up. However, the Corporal, who had more service than I had, had a wicked sense of humour. He said, "No, let them go on singing. That way we can be certain that the Provisional IRA won't open fire on us!"

One evening we were ordered to Fort Monagh. This was a Security Force Base (SF Base) that was on the road leading out of Belfast, up into the hills on the way to Hannastown, and out towards the airport. Nowadays it is a newly built housing estate, but in 1975 Fort Monagh was an old disused school off the main road. At that time, 40 Commando Royal Marines occupied it. They had arrested a young woman for throwing bricks at soldiers.

As we were not allowed to handle female prisoners, we drove out of Ardmillan House with a crew of three plus a member of the Women's Royal Army Corps (WRAC), known as "Coffeepots" to handle the prisoner. We collected the prisoner and drove off with her to Andersonstown RUC Station to hand her over to the police. When we got into Fort Monagh, we were directed to where two burly Marines were guarding a young woman. We listened to the story of how she got herself arrested and informed her that we were going to take her to the local RUC Station. At that moment, we became aware of a commotion outside the entrance to the base. It was the girl's mother and father asking about their daughter.

I went to the gate and explained that we would take the daughter down to the RUC Station, hand her over and it was then up to the RUC what happened next. Just then the Women's Royal Army Corps woman – with the female prisoner – came out of the building that they had been in.

"I will see you down at the police station," shouted the girl to her parents.

"Okay love," they replied.

Now one of my other crew members was a tall, well-built young man, single and good-looking, named Gary. With the step up into the Land Rover being a bit high, he moved forward to give the female a hand up. She turned on him and sank her teeth into the upper part of his arm. He gave a yelp and stepped back and the WRAC stepped forward. As she did, the female prisoner, not much older than 19, sat down on the tailboard and kicked the WRAC in the chest, sending her sprawling backwards to the ground. At this point, the WRAC had had enough. She launched herself at the female prisoner and knocked her backwards into the Land Rover. She then jumped in after her and all I knew was that there was a lot of noise going on. When I did look into the Land Rover the WRAC told us to get a move on and drive down to the RUC Station, as she sat on the prisoner to keep her in place. We quickly did so. Arriving at the RUC Station we dismounted from the Land Rover and made our way inside. The prisoner's parents were waiting on her arrival and when they saw their daughter's dishevelled, slightly battered condition, her father shouted, "Who did this to you?"

Without hesitation, the prisoner pointed at the young Corporal and shouted, "He did."

All hell broke loose. The RUC officers in the station had to come to our rescue and ended up arresting Dad, Mum and daughter for assault.

The Corporal turned to me and said, "I didn't do a thing." I agreed, as I had seen everything that had taken place.

When we got back to Ardmillan House, the Corporal took off his combat jacket to reveal his arm. The female prisoner had bitten right through his jacket and had left a lovely set of teeth marks on his upper arm.

One of the more pleasant facets of being on sentry duty at Ardmillan House was that there was a nice lady who lived across the road from the House. She would walk over during the evening and push a plastic bag under the gate with a cheery call of, "Here you go, son." The first time it happened to me I was inside the brick sangar and nearly jumped out of my skin. I told the Operations Room via the intercom what had happened, and they replied, "It's okay, the lady lives across the street. You will find a Thermos of coffee in the bag and a slice or two of cake. It's your lucky night to be on sentry when she turns up." This was another example of the two sides of the divide in Northern Ireland.

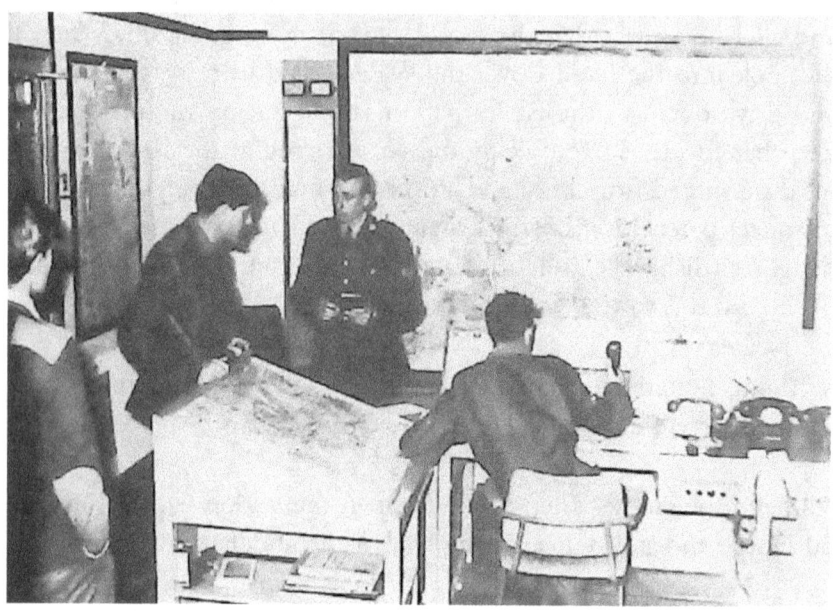

Company Operations Room, top floor of Ardmillan House

CHAPTER 7

Captain Black & The UDA

My dad was still the Quartermaster of Alexander Barracks in April 1974, when my wife Alison joined me in Northern Ireland. We lived in one of the sixty mobile homes on the edge of RAF Aldergrove. Ours was No. 57.

The mobile home was a big caravan with everything being small, like the kitchen, bathroom, front room, one bedroom, and a storage room. As the Northern Ireland folk would say, "You couldn't swing a cat in it." But for a young newly married couple like us, it was a start, and just in time, as in mid-April, Alison informed me that she was pregnant, and gosh, was I shocked. I know what you're thinking, "If you put your hand into the fire, don't expect it not to get burnt," but still, it was a surprise, as I did expect to have children sometime, but not just now.

Stupidly, I let my feelings show, and Alison was upset that I was not overjoyed at the prospect. A few weeks into her pregnancy, she began to show signs of distress, and after a visit by the local GP, she was taken to Lagan Valley Hospital in Lisburn, as she was on the verge of a miscarriage.

The doctor then informed us that things were not going well, that a termination was a possibility, but since terminations were not allowed in Northern Ireland, she would have to go back to England to obtain one. Then he added that he felt that "nature would take its course" and as it turned out, he was right. Alison miscarried towards the end of June. For me, I didn't know what to do or say; I just needed to be there for her. However, being beside her did not last long. I was called up for duty and sadly, I had to leave Alison by herself. There was no time off for looking after one's wife. It was simply a case of getting on with it. Off I went with the platoon.

It was about this time that the Royal Military Police was hit with two tragic incidents in a short space of time. The first example illustrated the strain some people faced and how seemingly mundane actions could take on greater significance when experienced first-hand.

A young female soldier who was working with the Royal Military Police was "going out" with one of the corporals – a chap named Fred. She went off on holiday and when she returned, she told the young Junior Non-Commissioned Officer that she had romantic ideas in another direction and ended the romance. One evening, as he was to go on patrol, the heartbroken young NCO withdrew his pistol from the armoury, loaded it, and then lay on his bed and shot himself in the head.

Another Junior Non-Commissioned Officer, ironically also named Fred, was the victim of slack procedures that left him maimed for life. His patrol was tasked to go and collect a weapon that had been found by the infantry during a search. He duly collected the weapon, but it had not been cleared by the Bomb Disposal people and a booby trap in it subsequently exploded, blinding him and blowing one of his hands off. The young man survived, and was going through rehabilitation when he suffered a heart attack which proved fatal. The coroner stated that the injuries he had received in Northern Ireland had largely been responsible for his death.

Chapter 7 - Captain Black & The UDA

For some reason best known to the authorities, it was decided that I should assume a post within the Royal Military Police HQ at the Operations Room within the RUC HQ at Ladas Drive in Castlereagh, Belfast. This was shift work and involved controlling all the 2nd Regiment Royal Military Police (2 RMP) patrols in Belfast by radio and telephone. It meant long days and even longer nights. As I was still new to the Province, I found it a bit of a struggle. Alison was still in hospital when, one evening after work, I was tasked with driving the civilian duty vehicle from Belfast back to Aldergrove, and I was told to take the Duty Clerk with me.

The Duty Clerk[16] was a single man and lived in the barracks, so in simple terms, all I had to do was to drop him off. When we reached the barracks, I asked the clerk, a private in the Royal Army Ordnance Corps[17] (RAOC), if he would drop me at home first so that I could take my car and get to the hospital to see Alison. He would then leave the vehicle in the car park for the next day's shift. He agreed to do so and dropped me off at home. He had only six hundred yards to drive back into camp.

About twenty minutes later, I drove into the barracks in my car to "book out" to see Alison in the hospital. As I drove in, I saw the duty vehicle parked by the side of the guardroom with the front smashed in! I went into the guardroom to ask what had happened, and I was told the clerk had collided with the gate post on turning into the barracks. The final sting in the tail was when the duty corporal informed me that the clerk did not have a driving licence!

The upshot of all this was that I was charged with negligence for not checking the clerk's driving ability, and I lost the job as Ops Staff and had to go back to the platoon. I tried to explain that I had been anxious to get to the hospital to see my sick wife, and that I had asked the clerk to drop me off. This cut no ice as it was held that, as he was

---

[16] An Army Duty Clerk in the British Army, or sometimes referred to as a Staff Clerk or Unit Clerk, handles administrative tasks and clerical work within the unit or headquarters.

[17] Royal Army Ordnance Corps were responsible for supplying weapons, ammunition, and equipment to the Army.

a private and I a corporal, my "asking" him was tantamount to an order that he could not refuse. I cannot remember how much I was fined, but the award of the Long Service and Good Conduct Medal (LS&GC) for 15 years" unblemished service was looking distinctly unlikely.

Company Duties Parade, Aldergrove 1973

As we approached 12 July,[18] there was the usual building of bonfires all over Belfast and the surrounding countryside. In our Operations Room (Ops Room) in Castlereagh RUC Station we had a large map on the wall that covered the whole of Belfast. It was printed in three main colours: orange for Loyalist areas, green for Republican areas, and yellow for mixed areas. Small logos depicting bonfires had been drawn all over this map, all in the orange areas.

---

[18] On the night before the Twelfth of July, or the Eleventh Night, bonfires are lit in Protestant/Loyalist neighbourhoods across Northern Ireland. The bonfires are a celebration of the Battle of the Boyne in 1690, when William of Orange defeated Catholic King James II. The bonfires are often accompanied by street parties and marching bands. The original beacons were lit to guide William"s forces to land.

Chapter 7 - Captain Black & The UDA

One evening, I was manning the telephones when a call came in. In a distinctly English voice, a man said,

"Are you aware of a very large bonfire at Grid Reference (GR) 123456 etc?"

I looked at the map and replied, "Yes, sir, we have that one."

The voice replied, "Okay, that's good, my name is Captain Black of the UDR."

Well, that's what I thought he said, because the Operations Officer (Ops O) then asked me, "Who was that on the phone?"

I replied, "Captain Black of the UDR."[19]

He replied, "No, that was Captain Black of the UDA![20] He keeps making calls into here to wind[21] us up. Next time, ask who is calling first, then you can hang up if it's Captain Black!"

I learnt very quickly that there were no manuals for working in Northern Ireland. I was to remain on a steep learning curve.

---

[19] The Ulster Defence Regiment (UDR) was an infantry regiment based in Northern Ireland that was part of the British Army. Formed in 1970, they were dissolved in 1992 and amalgamated with the Royal Irish Rangers to form the Royal Irish Regiment. The UDR was the largest infantry regiment in the British Army, with 11 battalions.

[20] The Ulster Defence Association (UDA) is an Ulster loyalist paramilitary group in Northern Ireland. During the 1970s they had a membership of 40,000.

[21] British/Irish slang meaning: to deliberately wind someone up or annoy them.

CHAPTER 8

Our First Red Cap Falls

The position of the Royal Military Police within Northern Ireland was a bit special. When you see films of the Troubles with troops in and around Belfast, they were all on "emergency" four-month tours. That meant that units could return repeatedly as the Troubles went on.

Security in Belfast city centre was controlled by an Army unit based in the old Grand Central Hotel (GCH). The Castle Court Shopping Centre now stands where it used to. From the Grand Central Hotel, all access to shops and "segments" in the city was controlled. The segments were areas of shops where all the alleys and side roads were blocked and secured with barbed wire so that there was just one access point, and that was controlled by either male or female soldiers, and some civilian "searchers." The female searchers had a particularly unpleasant job. They had to search the handbags, bodies, and clothes of women entering the segments. They recalled incidents when checking the pockets of coats to find used tampons and sanitary towels. They all wore leather gloves. Alternatively, there were sometimes broken razor blades in the pockets; somehow, the person wearing the coat forgot that such items were there. Not nice.

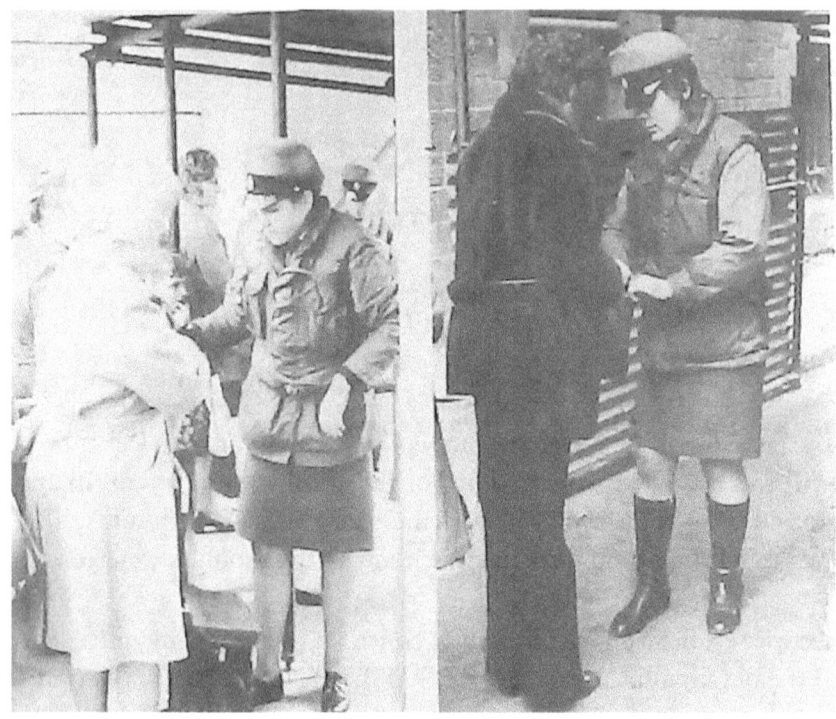

Women's Royal Army Corps (WRAC)
Searching the public as they entered the city centre

Lance Corporal William Jolliffe

Once we arrived in Northern Ireland, it would be for a two-year tour. We were not looked upon as "soldiers" like the rest of the British Army; we were not seen as police like the RUC either, so we tended to be somewhere in the middle. There were places we could go that the RUC could not, and places where we were accepted that the remainder of the British Army was not. For example, following an incident in Derry/Londonderry/Maiden City (whichever one you call it) at the start of the Troubles, one of our Land Rovers was attacked and petrol bombed. A young Lance Corporal riding in the back of the Land Rover was killed.

Chapter 8 - Our First Red Cap Falls

Extract from The Derry Journal:

> "A YOUNG BRITISH military policeman was fatally injured in an incident at the junction of Westland Street-Cable Street a few minutes before midnight yesterday morning. The dead man was Lance Corporal William Jolliffe, age 18, of Chippenham, Wiltshire. He was a member of 173 Provost Company of the Royal Military Police.
>
> He was one of three military policemen on routine patrol in the area. As the jeep reached the junction, a youth threw a petrol bomb, which did not explode but then a gang of youths numbering between 20-30 attacked the vehicle, which burst into flames, went out of control and crashed into a wall. The driver managed to get out, but the other two occupants were trapped in the vehicle. Residents of the area helped to extricate them and they were cared for in a house until an ambulance arrived. The badly injured soldier was taken to hospital, but he died soon after admission.
>
> A youth was arrested shortly after the incident.
>
> The army stated yesterday that the residents of the area had been very helpful after the incident and appreciated the care taken of the two injured men. The second soldier was stated to be suffering from shock.
>
> It was reported that some of the gang involved in the attack wore stockings over their faces. They made off over Cable Street.

Bishop's Condemnation

In a statement on the killing, the Bishop of Derry, the Most Rev Dr Farren, said:

> "I learned the horror of this terrible event in Derry, especially as things in this city seemed to be under control. I condemn, as I have already stated in my recent Pastoral Letter, actions of this kind, out of which no good can be expected to come." Dr Farren expressed his sympathy with the relatives of the dead soldier and added, "I hope and trust that this is not the beginning of new trouble but that it will bring people generally to realise that they have a big part to play individually in restoring order and peace to our city, especially in controlling the young."

John Hume MP condemned the incident. (Other than the first line, we are unable to decipher his comment.)

Chapter 8 - Our First Red Cap Falls

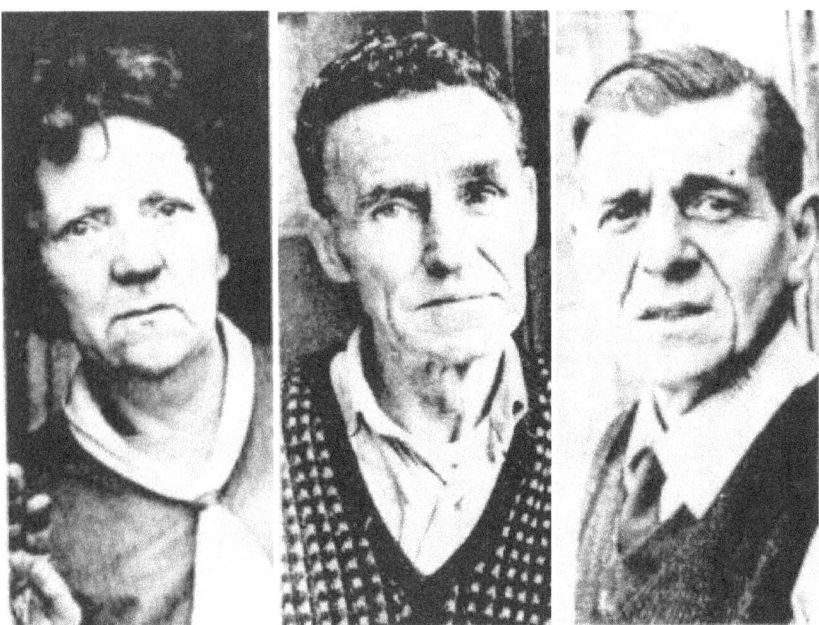

The three heroes of that day who tried to save the life of the soldier

Kathleen into whose home the soldier was taken after the attack.

Willie tried in vain to open the Land Rover door to rescue the soldiers after the attack.

Tommy also tried unsuccessfully to open the Land Rover doors after the attack.

Local newspaper reports the RMP soldier's murder

A message was sent from the "enemy" side, so to speak, that the attack was regretted and if the Royal Military Police would somehow designate their vehicles differently from the rest of the Army, they would try to ensure that we were not attacked again.

Our military commander in the city considered the offer and concluded, "If doing such saves one of my soldiers, then it is worth it." From then on, all Royal Military Police Land Rover patrol vehicles in Derry/Londonderry had Military Police plates on the sides of the vehicles as well as front and back, and the roofs were painted white. We never got directly attacked again. Doesn't that tell you something?

This story, like many secret deals done with the paramilitaries on both sides, has passed into the realm of "urban myth," but for this one, there are many still alive today who will testify to its authenticity.

CHAPTER 9

We Walked The Blocks

When internment was introduced, lots of suspected terrorists were held without trial in HMP Maze, or Long Kesh, as most of us knew it.

In the '70s, all this conflict was new, not just to us but also to the terrorists, so everyone was learning and adapting, sometimes on the spot. At first, terrorists would pick up a gun and fire it without wearing gloves, not realising that fingerprints could be taken if the weapon was recovered. They also did not realise that when a gun is fired, residue from the shot transfers onto the hands, clothing, and body. Later, they became more cautious, wearing gloves and boiler suits, and washing immediately after returning to a safehouse to remove any trace of forensic evidence. As terrorists became smarter, so too did we. This applied equally to the main prisons in Northern Ireland.

Crumlin Road Gaol, Belfast

Known locally as the *Crum,* it is now a Grade A-listed building because of its architectural and historical significance. Built between 1843 and 1845, it received its first batch of 106 inmates in 1846, who were forced to walk in chains from Carrickfergus Prison. During the early years, 17 prisoners were executed by hanging and then buried in the prison yard.

Later, as the Troubles erupted, suspected Republican and Loyalist terrorists were held on remand at the Gaol. On the day of their trial, they would be escorted through an underground tunnel[22] to Crumlin Road Courthouse, situated directly across the road. It has been stated that every convicted terrorist came through the Gaol.[23]

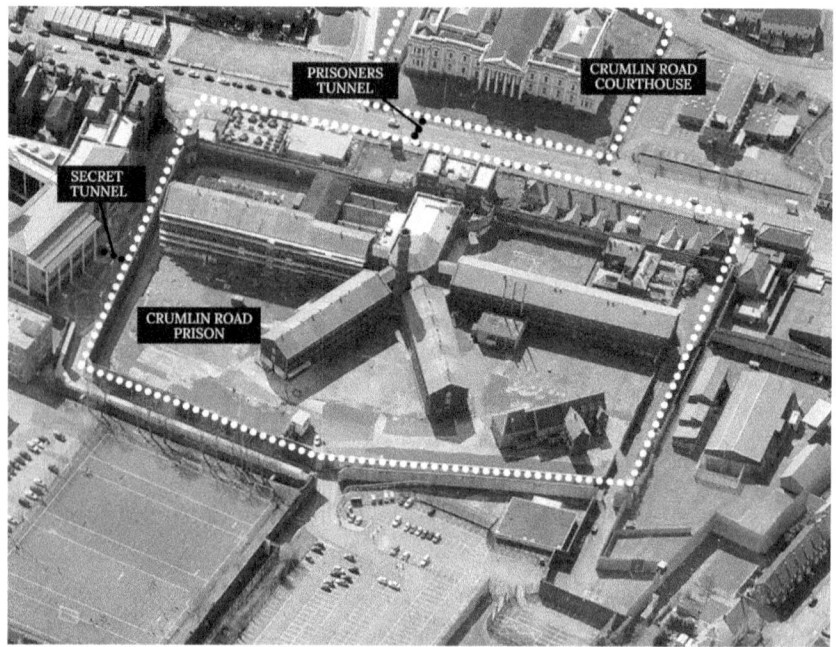

Crumlin Road Prison
(marked with dots)

In June 2023, workmen uncovered a secret tunnel leading from D wing of the Crumlin Road Prison under the road to the Mater Hospital. The tunnel, which has been blocked off just feet from the perimeter wall of the former jail, does not appear on any maps or drawings of the site.

---

[22] The tunnel can still be seen today.
[23] The Gaol is now a popular tourist attraction.

Some prison officers had mentioned a secret tunnel, but its existence was never confirmed, as no documents or site plans recorded it – until now.

The Department for Infrastructure later stated that it had been aware of the "decommissioned" tunnel and that it had been previously used to transport prisoners.

The secret tunnel from the prison to Mater Hospital,
discovered in June 2023
(Image by Justin Kernoghan)

HMS Maidstone Prison Ship

HMS Maidstone was a British prison ship used to hold IRA members and their supporters in Northern Ireland in the 1970s. Originally commissioned in 1937, she had a distinguished war career.

Maidstone was a submarine depot ship; her role was to resupply and refit the British submarine fleet in the Mediterranean and the Far East. She weighed 8,900 tons, carried a complement of 1,167 men and could steam at 17 knots. On board were a foundry, coppersmiths, plumbing and carpentry shops, electrical and torpedo repair shops, plants for charging submarine batteries and heavy and light machine shops.

In 1969, the ship was sent to Belfast to house 2,000 troops during increased security. For a while, it accommodated 179 Pro Coy Royal Military Police, commanded by my dad as OC of the company. Then, in 1971, it was hastily converted into a prison ship.

Among those living aboard was General Sir Mike Jackson, who would later become the head of the British Army. Another resident, less famous but more tragic, was Gunner Robert Curtis of the 94 Locating Regiment, Royal Artillery, who on February 6, 1971 became the first British soldier officially killed in the Troubles.

Later that year, the soldiers moved out and 122 IRA prisoners and supporters moved in.

The prison area was located at the stern and consisted of two bunkhouses (one up, one down), and two mess rooms. Above these were the rooms of the governor and his staff (formerly the captain's cabin), and above that was the deck, used twice a day for exercise. The deck was enclosed with three-metre-high barbed wire.

In January 1972, a group of IRA prisoners attempted a dramatic escape after someone noticed a seal swimming through the barbed wire surrounding the ship.

They greased themselves with butter and boot polish to squeeze through the ship's portholes and, wearing only their underpants, swam 270 metres across the ice-cold Belfast Lough.

Chapter 9 - We Walked The Blocks

Once ashore, they hijacked a double-decker bus before slipping across the border. Unsurprisingly, this was a propaganda coup for the IRA. The escapees, dubbed "The Magnificent Seven," even held a press conference in Dublin.

In April 1972, all internees[24] were moved to Long Kesh prison, including Gerry Adams.[25]

Internees, guards in a secured area on MS Maidstone 1970

---

[24] Civilians who are deemed as a potential threat and held without trial.
25 Gerry served time on the Maidstone and then in Long Kesh and to this day denies he was a member of the IRA, although his former colleagues would disagree, as would the family of Jean McConville – as told in "Say Nothing."

Prison Ship leaves Belfast for the last time

HMS Maidstone's spell as a prison ship lasted three years, after which she remained in Belfast to provide immediate short-notice accommodation for the Army in case reinforcements were suddenly needed.

Finally on May 23, 1978, she was towed to Rosyth in Scotland, where she was broken up for scrap.

HM Prison Magilligan, Limavady

HMP Magilligan first opened in January 1972, when 50 Irish Republican internees were transferred from the prison ship *HMS Maidstone*. The camp comprised eight Nissen huts on the site of a former army base. The prison was divided into compounds to house the various paramilitary internees. It was later modernised, and in 2017, Magilligan Prison was judged the best-performing jail in Northern Ireland, according to an unannounced inspection by the Criminal Justice Inspection Northern Ireland (CJI) and Her Majesty's Inspectorate of Prisons in England and Wales (HMIP).

HM Prison Magilligan, 1970s

HM Prison Maze, otherwise known as Long Kesh, H-Blocks

HM Prison Maze opened in the early 1970s, and by 1972 there were 924 internees. By the end of internment on 5 December 1975, 1,981 people had been detained: 1,874 were Catholics/Irish Republicans, and 107 were Protestants/Loyalists.

The disparity in these numbers has often been a source of contention.

However, it's important to consider the context of the time. Many violent incidents during the early stages of the Troubles were attributed to Republican paramilitary groups. As a result, security forces initially focused their efforts on addressing these activities, leading to higher detention rates among Catholic/Nationalist individuals.

This focus was not without its flaws, and the internment policy itself drew significant criticism for being imbalanced and, in many cases, unjust. But it reflects the reality of the conflict's early years, when Republican paramilitaries were responsible for many attacks, prompting a disproportionate response from law enforcement.

In July 1972 William Whitelaw introduced Special Category Status; anyone convicted of a paramilitary offence (a convenient phrase for "terrorists") would have it. Privileges included free association between prisoners, extra visits, food parcels, and the right to wear their own clothes rather than prison uniforms. But this was short-sighted, as these inmates believed they were not committing crimes, but acting for a cause. In turn the prison became a Prisoner of War camp (POW) where they held their own exercises, drills and weapon and bomb training. (Originally not with real weapons or bombs, but later they would). The Secretary of State for Northern Ireland, Merlyn Rees, ended Special Category Status on 1 March 1976.

With this book not being about Long Kesh I won't go into the "Dirty Protest," or the prisoners destroying their cell furniture, or the Hunger Strike, where they gave their lives while others of the same organisation wore suits and were on the MI5 payroll. Or the prison escape in 1983 – the biggest in British peacetime history. Thirty-eight prisoners hijacked a prison meals lorry and smashed their way out. During the breakout, four prison officers were stabbed, including James Ferris, who died of a heart attack. Another officer was shot in the head with a gun that had been smuggled in. The escapees injured several other officers. Nineteen of the prisoners were soon recaptured, but the other nineteen escaped across the border to their haven.

Chapter 9 - We Walked The Blocks　　　　　　　　　　　　　　85

HMP Maze, otherwise known as Long Kesh and the H-Blocks

PRISON SMUGGLING

How does someone smuggle contraband into a maximum-security prison? The answer lies in human psychology, careful planning, and split-second timing.

The Visiting Room Setup

Each prisoner was brought into a separate visiting room with a small table attached to the wall: one chair for the prisoner, with a Prison Officer standing directly behind him, and on the opposite side, two chairs for visitors. Simple enough – or so it seemed.

Contraband was smuggled in using everyday items. Chocolate bars, soap, toothpaste. The method was ingenious in its simplicity. Take a bar of soap, cut it carefully from side to side, hollow out a small cavity, insert whatever needs smuggling, then melt the soap back together. To any casual inspection, it looked completely normal.

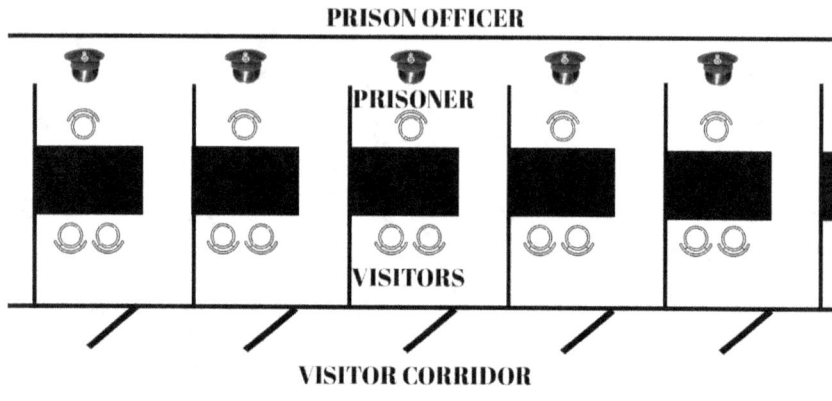

HMP Maze Visiting Room - where the deadly game was played.

Building Trust

The real skill was in handling the Prison Officers: treat them well over multiple visits, share sweets, offer cigarettes. Gradually, some officers began to relax their guard and started to see regular visitors as harmless, even friendly.

Then came the crucial moment. A visitor would offer the officer a sweet or a cigarette. In those days, smoking was permitted during visits. Everyone would light up – the prisoner, visitors, sometimes even the officer if he was a smoker.

"Do you have a light?" became the magic question.

Most officers didn't carry lighters. They'd have to ask a colleague, usually positioned about six feet away. The officer would walk over, get a light, and return. Those few seconds – maybe ten at most – created the opportunity.

The Transfer

While the officer's back was turned, contraband moved fast. A woman might retrieve something concealed on her body and pass it under the table. Quick, practised movements. By the time the officer returned with the lighter, everyone was sitting normally, smiling, waiting for their cigarettes to be lit.

The officer saw nothing suspicious. Just a normal family visit.

The Kiss

An even bolder method involved the farewell. As visiting time ended, the visitor would create a distraction.

"I think I hear Benny next door."

"I don't know," the prisoner would respond.

"I'm sure it is. Can you check?"

The prisoner would turn to the officer: "Could you see if that's Benny in the next room? Just to settle this."

The helpful officer would step around the corner for a quick look. In those brief moments, a bullet wrapped in plastic could pass from visitor to prisoner through what appeared to be an innocent goodbye kiss.

When the officer returned - "No, it's George." – he'd witness what looked like a normal farewell between family members.

Corrupt Officers

Some Prison Officers became part of the system, either through sympathy or fear. The sympathetic ones found it easy to walk contraband through security checks – after all, staff searches were far less rigorous than visitor searches.

Others were blackmailed: a phone call at home, details about their children's school, their wife's workplace, or their daily routines. These officers knew the people making threats had killed before and would kill again. The pressure was enormous.

Gradually, some broke. They began carrying small items through security. Once they'd done it once, there was no going back.

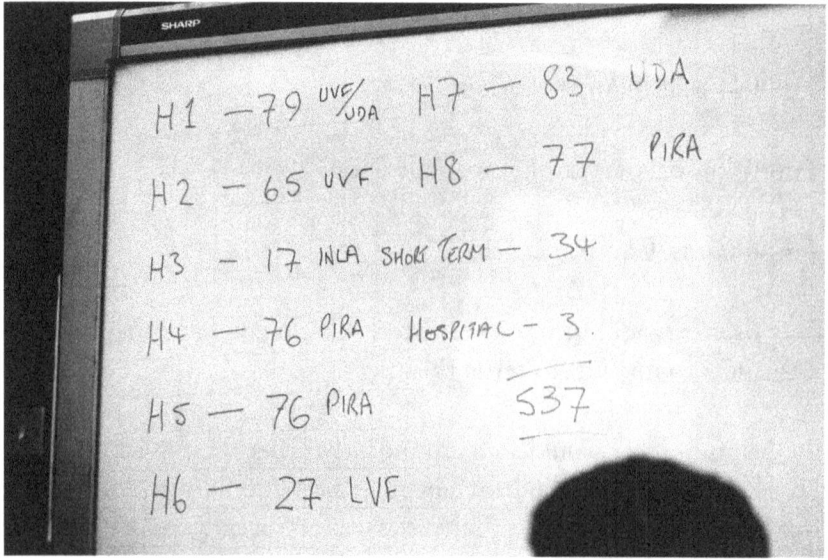

Number of terrorists being held in H-Block

Constant Vigilance

Prison searches became routine. Officers would tear apart cells, examine every possession, check ceiling light holders, and so forth. They knew weapons were getting through – they just had to find them before someone got hurt.

Every bar of soap was suspect. Every tube of toothpaste was potentially dangerous. In this environment, trust became a luxury no one could afford.

The visiting rooms remained battlegrounds where ordinary conversation masked deadly serious business. A handshake might conceal a transfer. A kiss might deliver death. In HMP Maze, even the most innocent human interactions carried the potential for violence.

Members of the 1st Regiment RMP searching HMP Maze in 1972

Members of the 1st Regiment RMP searching HMP Maze in 1972

Musgrave Park Hospital Security

Sometimes we in 175 Pro Coy got tasked with jobs outside our normal duties. One of these was providing security at Musgrave Park Hospital, which had a military wing and was where Long Kesh inmates were taken if they needed medical treatment or surgery. Appendicitis, minor procedures, that sort of thing.

We were told to provide security for this one Provisional – male, in for some surgical procedure. Got him into our Land Rover with three of us and off to Musgrave Park. Being on remand, these prisoners were allowed certain privileges. Visitors were one of them. Once we had him placed in his single-sided ward, we took turns standing at the entrance, checking anyone who came in or out.

Chapter 9 - We Walked The Blocks

During our 24-hour stint, nothing happened. Quiet as you like.

A few days after we'd finished, the prisoner had a visitor – his wife. Being female, the lads on duty couldn't search her properly, plus she wasn't allowed any bags in. They asked for a bit of privacy, maybe some hanky-panky we thought, so they were allowed to "talk" in the side ward with the door closed. Visit ended, all seemed well.

The next shift came on and, as normal, asked, "Was there anything needing reported?" When they heard about this private visit, alarm bells went off. They went straight to the prisoner and did a proper search of the side ward, turned him out of his bed, patted him down.

Nothing was found. But it's hard to beat experience. Even though everything looked normal, this officer's gut was telling him that something wasn't right.

As the prisoner stood there, the Redcap eyeballed him, then stepped back and ordered him to squat. The prisoner tried to convey the pain he was in, that this would be a struggle, but our man wasn't taking "No" for an answer.

"Squat!" he commanded again.

As the prisoner started to squat, a package dropped out from his backside.

What they found made everyone's blood run cold. It was a small .22 pistol, covered in tape and shoved between the cheeks of his backside, with the barrel tucked right in the crease. He had been lying there for hours, with a loaded weapon literally up his backside, waiting for his moment.

The Provo was arrested on the spot – a formality really – and all visits were stopped for the rest of his treatment. Under questioning, he admitted the plan: to wait until the early hours when security was lightest, produce the weapon, and force his way out. Simple as that. Walk out a free man whilst some poor sod bled out on the floor.

The thought of what could have happened if that shift hadn't been switched on still gives me the shivers. Three or four lads doing their job, thinking they're dealing with a sick man in a hospital bed. Instead, they're sitting ducks for someone with nothing to lose and a gun hidden where the sun doesn't shine.

As one of the lads said afterwards, "You just cannot trust anyone round here." Dead right. In that place, even the sick ones were planning to kill you.

* * *

Cage 27

The prison authorities referred to them as compounds, but the prisoners called them cages. Our raid was on the Republican Compound *Cage 27*. These actions usually took place at dawn: we'd arrive in the early hours when it was still dark, with local infantry securing the outer perimeter whilst we went in.

The drill was always the same. Each hut had to be entered simultaneously; otherwise, you lost the element of surprise. Anyone still in bed was ordered sharply: "Lie still, hands on top of the bedclothes!" No messing about. Once the prisoners were secured, the searchers went in.

Chapter 9 - We Walked The Blocks

Each bed space had an RMP Non-Commissioned Officer posted at the foot of it, armed with just a baton. No firearms. The prisoners were told to get up and hand over whatever clothes they wanted to wear. We'd frisk the clothes first, then they'd get dressed and be escorted to the dining hut.

This job fell to us because we were trained in search techniques, the same as any police force. There was also the problem that, if the infantry lads guarding us carried out the searches, things might go missing or get damaged. Military Police were better suited for this sort of work; that was the thinking, and it was probably right.

Once all the inmates were out, we photographed everything, then the real search began. Prison staff would come in at the same time to grab bits of contraband they'd spotted on previous visits but hadn't been able to reach.

The main thing was these bloody great tea urns – the type you might see at village fêtes. The inmates had kept hold of them and filled them with fruit, water, sugar – anything that would ferment into some kind of hooch. They stank to high heaven when opened. The warders would tip the lot down the drain and cart the urns off. They wouldn't normally come into the compounds for them – that was too risky. They had to wait until we were there to provide cover.

The strange thing was, because these prisoners were on remand awaiting trial, they were allowed certain privileges. Woodworking tools, would you believe: hammers, chisels, files, the lot. Perfectly legal. And they used them. You could find these spinning wheels in the lockers, beautifully made, all carved and varnished to professional quality. These got sold in the Prisoners' Aid Shops in Belfast. Where the money went…well, you can guess.

What really got to you were the wooden guns. Perfect replicas of Thompson sub-machine guns and pistols, all painted black or varnished. They could be stripped down part by part, just like the real thing. Teaching aids, basically. We could confiscate those, but not the spinning wheels. I knew a couple of lads who took their batons to the spinning wheels anyway, but most of us stuck to the rules.

Items displayed uncovered in Long Kesh by RMP

Hygiene wasn't their strong point. Strip a bed for searching and the sheets were always grey, sometimes nearly black. The crazy thing was, they'd often find sets of clean sheets tucked away in lockers. God knows why they kept them.

Chapter 9 - We Walked The Blocks

It wasn't pleasant work. Every time I left that place after a search, I felt dirty, not just from the physical filth, but from something else. The whole atmosphere in those cages was wrong. You could feel the hatred coming off them in waves, and it took a while to shake that feeling once you got outside.

As soon as duty ended, I went straight home, stripped off outside the front door, and threw my uniforms straight into the washing machine. Only after a long, hot shower with plenty of soap did I feel clean again.

On one occasion, in the middle of a search, a rumpus kicked off. When this happened, we pulled out of the huts and the infantry soldiers who were maintaining a cordon around the cages went in and subdued the disturbance. It was like standing in the middle of a film production, only the people were not acting.

I remember once, as all this was going on, I stood outside the cages watching bodies rushing in and out of the huts when I noticed a young captain next to me. Immediately, I recognised him.

Forgetting all military protocol, I said, "Captain Taylor, ex-Marlborough House, Duke of York's Royal Military school?"

He looked at me as if to say, "And who are you?"

I said, "Chipperfield, Kitchener, Wolfe and Wolseley."

"Of course," he replied, "how are you?"

So there we were – two "Dukies", old boys of the Duke of York's Royal Military School in Dover – standing in the middle of a compound in Long Kesh with a minor riot going on, reminiscing about what we had done and who we had seen since leaving school.

CHAPTER 10

"Rat Trap at Flak Jacket One-Over"

I was due two weeks' leave, and the wife and I decided to use it as a holiday to see Mum and Dad, who'd been posted to Hong Kong again. Using RAF transport, we flew from Aldergrove to London, then from Brize Norton via Akrotiri[26] in Cyprus and Gan in the Indian Ocean to Hong Kong.

Arriving in Hong Kong was brilliant – such a change from the stress I'd left behind. We had a great time in the sun, with good weather every day, and we saw all the tourist sights. We even dragged Mum and Dad round some of them.

But holidays don't last, do they? We returned to Northern Ireland, and I was straight back on patrol in Belfast. Sometimes, when things were kicking off in various parts of the city, the order would come over the radio:

"All callsigns, this is Zero, Rat Trap."

For us three in the RMP Land Rover, it meant throwing up a quick Vehicle Check Point at a location we called "Flak Jacket One." This was a disused petrol station on the Lisburn Road at the junction with

---

[26] RAF Akrotiri is home to the Cyprus Operations Support Unit, which provides joint support to British Forces Cyprus and to operations in the region, helping protect the UK"s strategic interests.

Blacks Road. It was perfect for our purposes – we could pull cars off the road heading into the city centre, give them a quick search and check, then let them back onto the main road.

We operated with one man controlling traffic, a second man checking the cars, and a third man providing security cover. My job was security at Flak Jacket One. Like a magician with his tricks, I'd just disappear. My thinking on covering VCPs was simple: better to be out of sight than standing there like a target.

Everyone went to their positions, and I heard, "Where are you, Chipperfield?" They were looking around, scanning the area, waiting for me to shout back. Eventually I called out, "Up here!" I was lying flat on the roof of the petrol station with a clear view of everything.

I remember this particular day. I'd been up on the roof for about fifteen minutes when I heard a voice with a northern England accent calling up to me:

"Oh lad, take this tray!"

There was this bloke at the back wall of the house next door, holding up a loaded tea tray: three proper mugs of tea and a couple of cakes. He introduced himself as Mr Hargreaves and said not to worry, the tea wasn't poisoned! He told me when we'd finished, just to leave the tray on the ground and his daughter would collect it.

As I took the tray, I called down to the lads, "Char up." They probably thought, what's he up to now? But when they came up to see what I was on about, they were well pleased.

After we'd finished the tea and cake, we got back to checking traffic.

Chapter 10 - "Rat Trap at Flak Jacket One–Over"

A few minutes later, this young woman appeared. A very tall, leggy blonde wearing hot pants and a tee shirt, walking this big shaggy Golden Retriever. Her blonde hair was so long it reached nearly to her waist. For the next few minutes, I don't think any of us was paying much attention to traffic control. It seemed to take ages for her to collect the tray and for us to thank her and her family.

From then on, we made damn sure we got Flak Jacket One whenever Rat Trap was called, hoping, of course, that Rosemary Hargreaves would come out to collect the tray again.

Oh, did I forget to say I got her name?

CHAPTER 11

Death Comes Looking

Part of our duties included patrolling East Belfast, which was loyalist territory. We had three Land Rovers with three to four men in each. One patrol at a time had to supply a guard to stand inside a sangar at Castlereagh RUC Station to back up the two-man guard on the front gate. On this particular day, I was in the sangar waiting for my relief.

Whilst I was waiting, thinking about what I was going to do later, not far from the station, the IRA burst into a house and had taken a family hostage. It wasn't random – the father drove lorries for a company that collected bound newspapers for recycling. When PIRA found this out, they held his family at gunpoint, loaded a bomb onto his lorry and ordered him to drive it to Castlereagh Station.

Castlereagh wasn't just any police station. It housed the Prisoner Reception Centre, where all terrorist suspects were brought for interrogation before being moved to Long Kesh. The IRA had decided to hit it.

The bomb got through security because the driver was well known to the gate guards. He came regularly to collect waste paper, so the lorry was waved through. Familiarity breeds contempt, as they say.

I'd left the sangar to use the toilet in one of our portacabins – the same one that had beds and armchairs for resting between patrols.

Suddenly I heard shouting and the sound of running feet outside. I walked to the end of the portacabin and opened the door, which swung outwards. As I did, it banged straight into the side of a lorry.

"Why would someone park so close to a door?" I thought.

I shouted at the first person I saw: "What's going on?"

"That lorry you just bashed into has a bomb on board!" came the reply from a fellow MP at the front gate, about fifty yards away.

Immediately, I ran to the sangar and got on the internal squawk box.[27]

"There's a lorry parked outside the portacabins with a bomb in it," I told the Duty Operator up in the Ops Room.

"Move it then!" he shouted back.

Might sound foolish now, but in that moment my thinking was: let me see if I can shift this thing. The thought of it going off never entered my head. Act first, think later – that was my mistake.

I ran to the gate to ask about keys, but they'd been removed, and the lorry had been allowed to stall. No chance of starting it.

Then I noticed someone in civilian clothes lying on the ground near the main gates, apparently fainted. I ran over to check him out, and he was just coming round. I asked who he was, and he told me he was the lorry driver. The IRA were holding his family hostage, he said, and had told him to drive the lorry into the station and leave it there.

---

[27] The term "squawk box" is associated with a non-lethal weapon, used by the British Army in Northern Ireland in the 1970s to disperse riots. This "squawk box" was an acoustic weapon designed to project high-frequency sound waves to incapacitate or disperse crowds.

He'd acted normally to get past the security team, then drove in and abandoned the lorry. Jumped out and tried to run for the main gate when he collapsed in shock. A couple of RMP NCOs from the gate helped him up and carried him to safety.

Then it hit me – right next to our portacabin was another one where the Intelligence Corps lads slept. I ran back into the yard past the bomb lorry but couldn't get into their cabin because the lorry was blocking the door. So I ran to the other end, gained entry, and found blokes asleep in bed. They'd locked themselves in for some peaceful kip.

I smashed the glass window of their room and shouted: "Grab your clothes, your ID, and get out the back door. There's a lorry bomb parked just feet from that wall!"

They didn't hesitate. In seconds flat, the portacabin was empty.

I ran back past the lorry again – to get to the sangar and report that I'd cleared the cabin. If I'd thought about it properly, I wouldn't have done that. Then I grabbed the patrol car belonging to the gate guards and drove it out of the station, leaving it across the main road to stop the traffic. I reported that the vehicle was parked across the road, but the Ops Room thought I meant the bomb lorry.

As I stepped out to speak to them on the squawk box, the bomb went off.

I stood there as a huge bundle of newspapers went up in the air and crashed down about ten feet from where I was standing.

The Aftermath

The lorry's chassis lay wrecked. The Intelligence Corps portacabin stood behind our battered RMP Land Rover, somehow still intact.

The bomb exploding at Castlereagh Station

What's left of the lorry on the right

Chapter 11 - Death Comes Looking

Bomb damage

Our own portacabin was obliterated, with nothing left but splinters and dust.

Both portacabins were destroyed. The Prisoner Reception Centre, the main target, had taken heavy external bomb damage. And yes, it was true. The IRA had held the family hostage.

Later that day I watched an Army bulldozer clear all the wreckage from the yard. One of the Int Corps blokes came up to me and said, "I've reported what you did to my OC. He says he's going to recommend you for something."

Nice thought. The problem was, our security had been breached, and the authorities reckoned they couldn't reward someone whose actions, noble as they might be, were only necessary because of a cock-up.

I could say I received nothing, but the truth is, I did. I lived to see another day.

CHAPTER 12

Arms Dumps Uncovered

I've always loved history. Wherever I go, I want to learn about the place. Take Templemore, for example. We patrolled through it many times. The name comes from Baron Templemore, a relative of the Chichester family, who once owned the land in and around Belfast. My curiosity led me to wonder why each house was finished differently, as I knew that after the Second World War houses were usually built uniformly to save money. I discovered that these homes had been built for newly arrived artisans and managers who had moved into the area to meet the labour needs of major employers. However, halfway through construction, Baron Templemore went bankrupt. Other builders then took over the work of completing the houses, which is why the avenue has so many different styles.

When we patrolled through the area, I always felt a sense of satisfaction knowing the history of those lovely homes. As I daydreamed about the past, wondering what it might have been like to live there, it was not long before I was brought back to reality...

I was in my usual position in the back of the Land Rover, seated on the floor with one foot braced against the towing hook on the outside of the vehicle and the other tucked underneath me for comfort. This way, I could scan the whole area to the rear of our vehicle for possible attacks.

As I scanned the area, I saw two men coming out of a house. One had his hand inside his jacket and, to all intents and purposes, looked as if he was hiding a weapon under his coat.

"Stop!" I yelled at our driver as I jumped out of the Land Rover, calling over to the two men, "You two," I said, "stop where you are."

They stopped and turned to face me. One man still had his hand inside his coat.

"Take your hand out of your coat slowly," I said. I won't tell you what they shouted back but it wasn't nice.

I then cocked my 9mm Sub Machine Gun (SMG) and pointed it at him. "Take your hand out of your coat very slowly or I will shoot," I said.

He now realised that I was not joking and removed his hand slowly, very slowly. My eyes were fixed on his movements, especially his hand. As it came out from behind his jacket, instead of revealing a pistol or suchlike, he revealed something I was not expecting: a fluffy kitten. He had kept it in the inside pocket of his coat to keep it warm. To prove it really was a kitten, he held it up by the scruff of the neck.

Whether I was in shock or full of adrenaline, I walked towards him and took the loaded magazine off my SMG. As I came up to him, I cracked him across the head with the magazine, which held thirty rounds. It was a demonstration of my anger and frustration at the man, and the amount of stress I was under, having nearly shot the idiot! He slumped to the ground with blood pouring from a head wound. I was very agitated. "You stupid git," I said, "you nearly got yourself shot for the sake of a kitten."

He said nothing. I got back into the Land Rover and told the driver to drive on. "Anything the matter?" asked my Sergeant from the front seat. "No," I replied, "just drive on." I was shaking like a leaf.

Similarly, one evening we were driving slowly along Mountpottinger Street, which led to the RUC Station in an area known as the Short Strand, a Republican stronghold. The night was dark and there was just one solitary streetlight on. As I watched out of the back of the Land Rover, I saw a figure hunched over the rear of a parked car in what looked to me like a firing position. I cocked my 9mm SMG and aimed it, when a childish voice shouted, "Bang! Got ya, mister." I must admit I did use some profane words as I, once again, unloaded my weapon and then put the magazine back on. It's no wonder some people got shot by accident.

One incident from this period stands out – although I wasn't personally involved. It was so extraordinary that it made it into *Reader's Digest*[28] as a textbook example of courage under fire and lightning-fast thinking.

Members of 175 Pro Company, my unit, had been deployed to a small republican stronghold on the Shore Road, which runs north to south on the city side of Belfast Lough. This was the Bawnmore Estate, fiercely republican territory where even the postman needed an armed escort.

Command had ordered a house-to-house search of the entire estate. What followed was an all-out gun battle between PIRA members and the Security Forces, the kind of firefight that turns suburban streets into war zones.

The team from 175 Pro Company had been attached to the infantry unit carrying out the search, tasked with processing any evidence or weapons uncovered. Leading our RMP team was Captain Len Murray (RIP), a Belfast man who served as Company Second-in-Command.

---

[28] *Reader's Digest* was founded in the US in 1922, while its first UK publication was in 1938. It contained articles like health tips, financial advice, and recipes. Unfortunately, the UK version closed down in 2024.

At the height of the gunfight, Captain Murray found himself trading shots with Provos, who were determined to make their stand. Suddenly, he spotted movement and rounding the corner of a house, came face to face with a gunman clutching a rifle.

Quick as lightning, Murray sprang up, levelled his pistol straight at the terrorist's chest, and bellowed, "British Army – hands up!"

Only then did his blood run cold. The slide on top of his pistol – the crucial part of the weapon's firing system – was locked to the rear with a round jammed solid in the chamber. His gun was completely useless. He couldn't have fired a single shot.

With nerves of steel and his heart hammering, Murray shouted again at the gunman. To his enormous relief, the terrorist lowered his weapon and raised his hands in surrender.

The gunman was immediately arrested, and Captain Murray quickly sorted out his jammed pistol – just in case the shooting started up all over again.

Arms dump uncovered, Bawnmore Estate, Belfast

Chapter 12 - Arms Dump Uncovered

One sunny day we were driving out of East Belfast, intending to cross the Albert Bridge, when a radio message came in about a vehicle stolen in the city centre some ten minutes earlier. On this occasion, I was the front seat passenger as my sergeant decided he wanted to drive for a change. As usual, I wrote the registration number on the windscreen with a Chinagraph pencil and, glancing up, was just in time to see the vehicle coming towards us over the bridge. It made a sharp left turn into the Short Strand area and tried to get away. My sergeant, a tough Scot and ex-Para, was not having it. He put his foot down and gave chase.

The car slowed to go over a ramp and we hit it from behind, shoving it forward until it stalled. We then rammed into the driver's door. We all leapt out, cocking our weapons as we went, and managed to collar and arrest both occupants. I informed our OPs room, which contacted the RUC. They sent out a patrol to take the car thieves off our hands. We had only been there about five minutes when the usual "rent-a-crowd" turned up and started giving us a bit of hassle. "What you got them two boys for?" "You let them go ya British…," and so on. Luckily, the RUC took over and asked us to ferry both prisoners to the RUC Station. The stolen car was recovered back to the station as well, and we got a "well done" from our Commanding Officer. Not a bad day, really!

On the question of weapons and their recovery: if the soldiers on the ground found one, it was up to us to collect it, take down all the details of place, date and time and then hand the weapon over to the RUC.

Arms Dump Find, Springfield Road, Belfast

One morning we were tasked to go to an address on the Springfield Road in Belfast, where an infantry patrol had found a rifle propped up in a small outhouse at the back of a house. We turned up and as I was by then an "old hand," I went to investigate. The weapon was a long rifle with a wooden foregrip, a wooden butt, and a magazine already fitted. I prided myself on being good at weapon identification – it had become my speciality – but I did not recognise this one.

Mindful of the risk of booby traps, I tied a long rope around the barrel, careful not to disturb it in case a pressure switch had been placed under the butt, and then retreated down the alley. A gentle pull on the rope sent the rifle clattering onto the path. It did not explode, nor did the impact set it off. I then undid the rope and took hold of the rifle. I had never seen one like it before, either in reality or in our weapon identification books.

I located the safety catch and applied it. Then, finding the magazine catch, I pressed it and removed the magazine. All the while I wore gloves, since plenty of forensic evidence could be lifted from weapons. Inside the magazine, I recognised the rifle rounds: 7.92x57mm Mauser cartridges from the Second World War. They had brass cases and nickel-coated bullets with a rounded rather than pointed tip.

A real expert's rifle. The IRA had been supplied with Mausers many years earlier, but although these were Mauser rounds, the rifle itself was a Swedish-made copy produced under licence. One or two of the soldiers involved in the find said they were sure they had heard it being fired in the area a few nights before. The high-velocity crack of its bullet was very different from the low-velocity thump of the Thompson submachine gun.

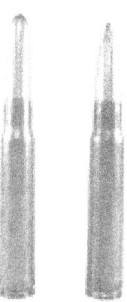

7.92x57mm Mauser round

CHAPTER 13

Boys Will Be Boys

From time to time, there were incidents that, even with the passage of time, still make me smile.

We had attached to our section a staff sergeant who had been a weapons-training Senior Non-Commissioned Officer (SNCO)[29] when I was in training at the Royal Army Physical Training Corps. He was very keen, and the only picture I can paint of him is this: if you are old enough, then cast your mind back to the programme *M*A*S*H*, which was on our televisions from 1972 to 1983.

From time to time in that show appeared a character named Colonel Flagg, supposedly from the CIA or FBI or some "secret" organisation. He was very "*gung-ho* (ready to fight), and could I say, a bit crazy. Our staff sergeant was in a similar vein. When we went on the shooting range, he would say things like, "You must kill the enemy; you have a pistol with ten rounds in it, make sure that when the yellow hordes stream over the hill you get every one of them. You are defending Western democracy."

Keeping his character in mind, we were once sent to an address way out in East Belfast, somewhere near Newtownards. As far as we were concerned, it was friendly territory. As we dismounted from our vehicle,

---

[29] SNCOs are experienced leaders who manage units, companies, and administration. They also train their units, focusing on marching, uniform standards, and behaviour.

our own Gung-Ho jumped out of the front passenger seat with a flourish. As he did so the magazine of his 9mm pistol fell out, hit the ground and the base plate came off, sending ten 9mm rounds scattering all over the place. Apart from laughing, we all began to look around to recover the rounds, but we could only find nine of the ten.

We noticed some boys aged about nine or ten playing nearby, and when they saw us searching, they came over to us. One of our blokes suddenly had a brainwave and said, "If you boys can help us find a bullet, we will give you 50p." The boys started scouring the ground and one approached us, but we couldn't believe what came out of his mouth: "My dad has some bullets like that in our house. He keeps them inside the Hoover."

Well, as that old saying goes, "opportunity knocks just once." A team of us then followed the boy to his home and chatted to his mum. We told her we had reason to believe that arms and/or ammunition were in the house and under the current NI law, we were going to come in and carry out a search. We, of course, made a show of looking everywhere and then picked up the hoover, opened it, and found inside it twenty rounds of said 9mm ammunition!

We then sent a message to HQ informing them of our "find" and we were told to stay put until an RUC patrol arrived. They turned up just as the young boy's dad, having been summoned by his wife, arrived home. We handed the ammunition over to the RUC, who promptly arrested his dad and took him away. We said nothing to the boy's parents about how we found the rounds and just hoped that the young lad kept his mouth shut.

I can also confirm that the missing 9mm round was later found, which was just as well, because "Gung-Ho" would otherwise have had some explaining to do.

Chapter 13 - Boys Will Be Boys

Just a few weeks ago, I was in Belfast city centre, standing at the bus stop in Donegall[i] Square East, waiting to catch the 9E bus back to Boucher Road to collect my car from its servicing at the dealer. I glanced behind me and noticed the "white" church. It is a distinctive building with a Greco-Roman front and a portico supported by long white pillars.

As I stood there, I recalled that back in 1974-1976, we used to drive around Donegall Square, in which stood Belfast City Hall, on several occasions when we were moving from base to base. I remembered that the vicar of that church during the Troubles kept a board mounted on one of the columns. It looked very much like the board in some churches to display hymn numbers for the congregation, but the priest used it to update the number of people who had died each day. We could go around the square in the morning and it might read XXXX5, and by the evening XXXX9, reflecting the latest casualties. I once saw a TV report of him climbing a ladder to change the figures. The saddest, most macabre moment came when he had to add another number to the figures. That number was reflecting the loss of his own son.

For further interesting information

[i] See endnote.

CHAPTER 14

The Dark World of Informing

For those of you who may not know what an informer is– or, as locals would call them, tout or grass – let me paint a picture.

An informer is someone who betrays their own side, selling out comrades to the enemy for money, revenge, or basic survival. In Northern Ireland, this meant Republican terrorists secretly feeding intelligence to the very security forces they were supposed to be fighting. Or Loyalists handing over their own for cash or a shortened sentence.

By the later years of the Troubles, it was widely known that the security forces had infiltrated every terrorist group in Northern Ireland. The scale was staggering – it's been suggested that one in three IRA terrorists were informers. Even those whose job it was to hunt out informers were sometimes themselves informers. Imagine being part of an Active Service Unity (ASU) on the way to carry out a killing: the driver, the front passenger, the man in the back seat. If you are not the informer, which one of them is? This was one of the main reasons the IRA eventually surrendered: the British had beaten them from within.

These informers "turned" for different reasons. Some craved the excitement, the adrenaline rush of living a double life. Others did it for cash – thirty pieces of silver in modern form. Many became disillusioned with their own organisation's brutality. And some were simply caught and turned by skilled handlers who knew exactly which buttons to press.

A good Military Police Officer was trained to extract information without the target even knowing they'd given it away. Clever questioning, casual conversation, reading between the lines. The informer would walk away thinking they'd given nothing away, whilst their handler had just learned about next week's operation.

The Force Research Unit had secret rooms scattered across Northern Ireland, and even in Dublin and Donegal. These were safe houses, or disguised rooms within houses, designed to look like ordinary homes. It was in these settings that the shadowy wing of military intelligence ran agents like pieces on a chessboard.

Communication was an art form. Code words were woven into everyday chat – it might be a colour, a cut of meat, or traffic conditions. It sounded innocent enough to anyone listening, but to the trained ear, it was setting up the next meeting. "The weather is not great today," could mean, "Too dangerous to proceed."

More than a dangerous job

Being an informer was the most dangerous job during the Troubles. Discovery meant certain death – usually after hours of "questioning" that would make grown men scream. These people lived double lives every single day, one slip of the tongue away from a shallow grave.

But they kept doing it. Kept taking the risks. Kept supplying information that saved lives and prevented attacks. And yet, other times, the Force Research Unit would allow operations to go ahead, as the informer was worth more to them alive than members of the UDR, RUC, Army, or even civilians. If you have the slightest doubt about this, consider the Omagh bomb, where 29 people and two unborn children were murdered, and 220 were injured. Why would the Special Detective Unit (SDU) of the Garda Síochána (Irish

Chapter 14 – The Dark World of Informing

National Police) monitor the location where the bomb was being built and watch the car leave to cross the border with fake Northern Ireland number plates?

The reality is that the Omagh bomb was constructed in the Republic of Ireland, in County Monaghan, before being driven across the border to its devastating destination. On 13 August 1998, a maroon Vauxhall Cavalier was stolen from Carrickmacross, County Monaghan. The Real IRA loaded this vehicle with 500 pounds of fertiliser-based explosives, replaced its Republic of Ireland number plates with fake Northern Ireland plates, and on Saturday 15 August drove the bomb car from County Monaghan across the Irish border to Omagh. Intelligence agencies on both sides of the border had informants within the Real IRA. Yet the bomb was assembled, transported, and detonated with devastating effect. The question remains: how much did they know, and when did they know it? The families of the victims deserve answers about why intelligence that could have prevented the deadliest single incident of the Troubles was not acted upon.

The following account[30] shows what it was like to be an informer during the Troubles.

The Wait

You're standing there, right?

Heart hammering out of your chest. Watching every light, every shadow. Listening for tyres on gravel. You don't know if you're about to be lifted, shot, or become one of the disappeared.

---

[30] For obvious legal and safety reasons, this account cannot be attributed to any specific individual or operation. However, it accurately reflects the methods and moral pressures that defined informer recruitment and their hidden life during the Troubles.

Then it comes: the van. Quiet. Pulls in at the prearranged location, the edge of a disused garage. The side door cracks open, and next thing, you're bundled in like a sack of spuds. *Bang.* Door shuts. You're gone.

Your life is now in their hands. No words. No faces. Van interior blacked out. Could be forty minutes, could be an hour, or maybe more. You might just be driven in circles, all to mess with your head. All the time you're being watched by another man, sitting on his arse just far enough away from you, with a pistol in his hand.

Then the van stops. You hear bars being dragged back, metal screeching like a warning. The van moves forward a bit, then stops again.

The front seat passenger jumps out and opens the side door of the van, issuing one word: "Out!" Feet hit the concrete. The smell hits hard – diesel, damp, oil, stale sweat. The place is a kip.

You're in a garage. Big, cold, dark, with a single light bulb flickering from the ceiling. A fella slides steel bars across the inside of the garage door. Greasy hair, a sandpaper face and don't mention his clothes: they have not seen water for weeks. He doesn't look at you. Doesn't need to.

The other three – the ones who brought you in – hover nearby. Not bored. Watching. Waiting. Making sure you don't bolt or make a quick move. Not that you were carrying;[31] they had already patted you down when you entered the van.

A door opens into the house. A man's voice calls, "In here."

---

[31] Expression for a weapon hidden on the body.

Chapter 14 - The Dark World of Informing

Image courtesy of Peter Moloney Collection

Tea and Biscuits

You follow the voice. You're led into a dated kitchen – yellowed tiles, an old cooker humming. Then through to the living room. He points to an armchair. You sit.

The table's already set. Steam rises from the teapot. Two mugs. Fig rolls on a plate, no expense spared. Feels like the last time a priest had called at my parents' house.

An electric fake fire was on, glowing, but the actual heat was turned off. I asked, "Can you switch on the heater?" The answer came immediately, without thought, "You'll soon be warm enough." Even that reply started to make me sweat. Family photos on the wall – but of whose family? Probably not his.

He starts soft.

"How are you keeping?"

"Your sister still waiting on the operation?"

"Craigavon Hospital, isn't it?"

"Aye," I said.

It wasn't chit-chat. It was flexing. Letting me know what they knew – that they could reach anyone close to me if I even sneezed the wrong way.

Then he asks, "What about Sean?"

Sean's the same rank as me. We work closely. I nod. "He's doing rightly."

Then came the kicker.

"What about John?"

Just like that, my stomach drops. *John?* What do they know? What don't they know? This wasn't curiosity; it was a test. A wrong answer could mean a hole in my head. It was about seeing if I'd talk, and what detail I'd give.

Operation

You see, I was trusted to escort comrades over the border. John – aka *The Executioner* – was wanted for murder in the North. He was lying low in Monaghan, under the Republic's "wink and a nod." My job was to collect him from a rebel pub.

Chapter 14 - The Dark World of Informing

Let me explain, you don't just walk into a rebel pub in Monaghan unless you belong. One wrong move and you'd be leaving in a bag. Strangers are spotted in seconds. Undercover soldiers rarely last long. One guy, Robert Nairac, sang rebel songs and all, but he was clocked – he didn't belong.

I ordered a drink and waited. The place looked ordinary: ashtrays full, empty glasses, rebel music, smoke hanging in the air. I sipped slowly.

Then a waitress who was collecting empty glasses came over and we had general chit-chat, including "Can I take your empty glass?" Then, under her breath, she said, "Go to the men's toilets." She continued collecting empty glasses, leaving the odd one still on the tables and then disappeared through a door in the side of the bar.

I waited a few minutes, then headed for the toilets. Two men were loitering in the corridor. I nodded, walked past, and entered the toilets.

Inside, three cubicles: one door hanging off, one closed, one open. No one in sight.

I stood at the urinals.

Then the closed cubicle door opened.

No name. Just: "Follow me."

We walked out. The two men followed us. Down a corridor and into a grubby room. Cigarette ash everywhere. Stank.

Another man stood near a door, chatting to a woman wearing a fur coat, headscarf, legs crossed, sitting on the sofa.

She turned her head around to me and said, "So, it's you who is taking me out for the day!" I tried not to let it show, but being honest, my mouth felt like it had dropped to the floor; it was John dressed as a woman, lipstick, handbag, and all. John put his hand up to me as to help him off the settee and in a squeaky voice said, "I'm Mary." I just shook my head.

One of the lads handed me the car keys. "Take the car out the back. Use this route. Don't stop."

We slipped out the back and as we were getting into a not-too-fancy car. John stood outside the passenger door and said, "Are you not going to open the door for me?" I won't tell you what my reply was.

Switching on the engine, I could see black smoke via the rear mirror rising from the exhaust. No terrorist would choose this for a mission. Which is why it was perfect.

We drove to the border. No issues at the Garda checkpoint. I nodded at the officer; he waved us through.

At the British Army checkpoint, surveillance would already have read the car plates and checked the car's owner from a distance. And now, we are in the queue waiting to be waved forward. Some cars were waved through the checkpoint, others moved to the side to be searched and so forth. It was now our turn as the soldier waved us forward.

We pulled up alongside him. The soldier leaned in.

Before he said anything, I said, "How are you doing, sir? It's not a bad night?" All for one purpose, to cause him not to feel threatened, that we were the "goodies." If only.

Suddenly, the baby on John's knee – sorry, Mary's knee – started to cry as if in pain. The soldier asked, "What's wrong with the baby?"

"Trying to get home, the wee soul is hungry," I replied.

With a smile, the soldier said, "Then you better get the baby fed. On you go."

We drove out of the security zone and into the dark. In less than 15 minutes, we had reached the safe house, a Republican home outside Newry.

The outside light on the right corner of the house was on and the top pane of a window was open…that was our sign that it was safe to stop.

By now the baby had fallen asleep. John gently lifted the baby out of the car, and we entered through the back door of the house, which had been left unlocked.

John removed his headscarf, which was covering most of his head. The local IRA commander laughed, "Only you, John. Maybe next time, shave your legs."

We all laughed. Tea was poured. Small talk. Nothing useful said – not in front of me. The real talk would happen after I left.

Then, a knock at the back door and a woman entered, saying, "I see the border crossing went well. Can I have my child back now?"

The 15 minutes we'd had the baby with us? That was our insurance policy. The baby wasn't hungry. John had pinched the baby to make it cry – to play on the soldier's empathy.

As the woman was leaving with her baby, the commander said, "Thanks, I'll be in touch again."

Then he turned to me, nodding towards the door, "Time for you to go." I left my tea untouched and slipped out the back.

Job done. We returned the car to its hide.

Back to Reality

A week later, I stepped out of a corner shop in Newry with a packet of smokes. As I lit up, I saw the same car I used to bring John over. Same number plates. A couple of dents in the same area on the car I had driven.

I learned two things: the vehicle I had driven was matched a vehicle that belonged to a Catholic who was above suspicion. And I was only told what I needed to know. Nothing more.

Back to the living room

Now you see why I nearly choked when the handler asked about John. I replied, "Yes, John's fine."

He offered me a biscuit. "No, thanks."

"Oh, go on, the tea will be too wet without one." Nothing for it but to take one.

It was a test, another hook. He was reeling me in. Teasing out details. Hinting at good money.

By the time we finished, the ashtray was full. I hadn't noticed how many smokes I'd gone through. Fear does that.

Then, as direct as he could be:

"You brought the sniper over the border?"

With no hesitation whatsoever, I replied, "Yes."

"You dropped him outside Newry?"

As I replied, "Yes." I could feel the cold sweat running down my back, and the fire wasn't on.

"You didn't see anyone else?"

"No."

"And the car?"

"I left it in the car park on the edge of town. Keys under the mat."

"And all that's true?"

I nodded. "Yes."

"Alright," he said. "I'll see you out."

"Those guns." He spoke. Looks like I'm not leaving yet, as I replied, "What guns?"

"At our last meeting, you suggested we take a look inside an old, abandoned slurry tanker that had basically never been used for years. We found it buried under bushes, thistles and so forth."

My reply was simple, "And?"

"We have it sorted." That was all I heard. I never asked, "Sorted in what way?"[32] I was not there to ask questions, only to provide answers.

As we stepped into the garage, he slipped an envelope into my hand. "Something for your trouble."

I climbed into the van. No one spoke. The rusted bar was drawn back. The garage door creaked open. The engine started. We reversed out.

I left that place not knowing where I'd been or if I'd ever see it again.

It would be years before I realised that it had been a secure location inside a British Army camp, designed to look like a family home. The only difference was that the rooms were bugged, every word recorded. When the handler made an excuse to visit the restroom, he was actually consulting with the Force Research Unit, which operated a full surveillance suite in the room next door. Nothing was as it seemed.

***

Rosslea, County Fermanagh

While based in Rosslea, our job was to talk to people and to find out who was going where and why. That and any other useful information would be sent up the chain of command to the intelligence boys, the Force Research Unit.

---

[32] Security forces placed tracking devices on or in weapons to monitor their whereabouts.

Chapter 14 - The Dark World of Informing

During my first tour at Rosslea, there was an Irish-registered car, the old black-on-red registration number, which crossed the border from the south to the north every Tuesday and Friday evening, and had been doing this for a long time.

If we were stopping the vehicles and this car was one of them, I couldn't resist asking each time, "Where are you going to?" The answer from the man was always the same: "Up the town for a drop for myself and a drop for the car." This translated as a few pints of beer and filling the car with petrol, as the petrol station was the nearest to where he lived. Anyone in the intel side of things will always be looking for a soft spot to manipulate for the purpose of extracting information.

I had noticed that the tax disc on this car was out of date, which I knew could cause him to be fined, so I mentioned it to the driver.

I said to him, "I am not interested in telling the RUC about your tax being out of date, but you should be careful when coming up north." He then told me, "My car is not only untaxed but uninsured as well, as I cannot afford to do it, as I am not working currently."

We radioed our base with his car's registration number.

Those who would be identified as either in a terrorist group or a supporter of such a group would be flagged up on our base computer once the car registration was submitted. The data would tell us who owned or was associated with the car, who would be expected to be in the car and if any of the people carried rank or were high risk to us.

The report came into my earpiece; his name identified him as a "volunteer foot soldier" with an IRA unit in the south.

I reported this information further up my chain of command and nothing else occurred during that duty.

Some twenty weeks later, on my next tour of duty at Rosslea, I was informed that a civilian car with a certain registration would come into the checkpoint late in the evening. After checking the identification documents of the sole driver, I was to direct him through the gates and into our compound. On getting out of the vehicle, the man asked for me by name and, once our mutual identification had been confirmed, he revealed that he was from 14 Intelligence Company (14 Int), a special forces undercover unit of the British Army that conducted covert operations during the Troubles.

This had been the unit that had run the "4 Square Laundry", a dry cleaning service that collected laundry from addresses in West Belfast connected with the IRA, and before returning the laundry washed and clean, had it scoured with the help of the forensic authorities for evidence. By collecting clothes of suspected members, British intelligence could inspect them for gunpowder residue, blood, gun oil and explosives. Important information was gathered, analysed, and then the clothes would be returned the following week, just like a normal laundry service.

A lot of information was gathered by this operation through various means, from the van driver chatting to locals, to comparing laundry lists. For example, if a woman's husband was known to be dead or in prison, but she was washing men"s clothing, then it could belong to a hidden IRA member. Unfortunately, the two undercover operators had their cover blown and the laundry van came under attack one day in the Twinbrook area of West Belfast.

Sapper Edward Stuart, the driver, stayed in the vehicle and kept a lookout, while his van helper, Lance-Corporal Walker, had gone to the front door of a house to return the customer's clothes, when terrorists launched the attack on the van.

Chapter 14 - The Dark World of Informing

"4 Square Laundry — Dry Cleaners" van

A car drew close to the van and three gunmen got out, whilst the driver remained in the car ready for a quick getaway. Sapper Edward Stuart was killed instantly by automatic weapons, thought to be Kalashnikovs recently supplied by Colonel Gaddafi of Libya.

At the first sound of gunfire, Lance-Corporal Walker faced the terrorists and engaged them with her 9mm Browning HP automatic pistol, forcing them to flee in their car.

Plain-clothes officers from the Royal Ulster Constabulary (RUC) in an unmarked car quickly arrived and secured the area.

Lance-Corporal Walker was awarded the Military Medal for her bravery.

Sapper Edward Stuart dressed in his undercover clothes
Murdered October 2, 1972

CHAPTER 15

Upholding The Law

One of the advantages of the Royal Military Police personnel doing two-year tours in Northern Ireland was that occasionally a court case would come up that you had been involved in and, rather than be called back from your next posting, you were able to attend court whilst still in the Province. Such was the case one day when I received notice that I was to be present in Belfast Crown Court to give evidence of my involvement with the detaining of an IRA man who had escaped from the Crumlin Road Gaol and had subsequently been recaptured. I was the Royal Military Police Non-Commissioned Officer who had re-arrested him from the infantry who had captured him, and for continuity of evidence, I had to be present to give my side of the story.

On the court day, I was working from our base in Tennant Street, just off the Crumlin Road, and I would have to appear in civilian clothes, naturally, so I arranged to take with me on duty that morning a suitable set of civilian clothes. I was also required to be armed and not having my shoulder holster, I drew one from our stores. It was a pathetic plastic thing, all straps and buckles, but did not secure very well and I did not have a good feeling about it.

The plan was that one of the patrols from my platoon on duty in Tennant Street would drive me the short distance to the Crown Court and would park around the back, thereby concealing someone in civilian clothes getting out of an Army Land Rover. As it turned out, the patrol due to do this got tasked to go somewhere else and the only alternative was for me to walk to the court.

It is not far from Tennant Street to the old Crown Court on Crumlin Road and as I was armed, my Platoon Sergeant was happy for me to walk off on my own. I made my way down to the Court with no incident or problem. As I walked in via the main entrance, the blokes on security duty, who were from my platoon, decided to have a bit of fun. As I approached, one of my mates stopped me and said,

"Is Sir a witness in a case today?" "Yes, Sir bloody well is." I replied. "Oh, if Sir wants to take that attitude, we can strip and search you, Sir and really mess up your day." I responded with, "Thank you, Corporal. I will just go in unmolested if it's okay with you?"

He was grinning all over his face as he said, "Carry on."

I entered and sat in the court's foyer, having given my name to the Court Usher. About 30 minutes later, the call went out, "Call Corporal Chipperfield," repeated once or twice for everyone's benefit. I was directed into the witness box and made the "I promise to tell the truth, etc." oath.

In Northern Ireland, witnesses now give their evidence from a seated position. Having taken the oath, I was directed by the Prosecution lawyer to "take a seat." As I leaned forward to park my backside on the chair, the lousy shoulder holster failed to do its job and a fully loaded 9mm Browning pistol fell out into the dock, making a very loud clatter as it fell to the floor.

The defendant, call him Mr Maguire just for now, looked across at me and smiled, and all his Republican relatives up in the public gallery leaned forward to see what had happened. Sheepishly, I retrieved the pistol from the floor and placed it back into my shoulder holster, making sure I clamped it there with my left arm.

The prosecution lawyer opened his questioning.

"Corporal Chipperfield, I put it to you that you were on duty in North Queen Street on the morning of blah blah blah."

"No, sir," I replied, "I was on duty in Tennant Street when I was tasked to go to North Queen Street."

At this, the learned judge looked over his spectacles at the prosecution lawyer with a smile on his face and said, "Perhaps that will stop you from asking leading questions, Mr Gillespie?" "I am indebted to your Lordship," said the lawyer, as he glared at me! I thought, "This is not going well."

After stating that I recognised the defendant and that I had taken custody of him and escorted him to the Prisoner Reception Centre at Castlereagh, I could leave. Luckily, that was the last case of the day, and the lads gave me a lift back up to Tennant Street, where I got changed back into uniform and continued as if nothing had happened.

With the duties that I was required to do, I did not get that much time off for relaxation, or any socialising with my wife, Alison. There were just one or two exceptions to this. The Royal Military Police were also stationed in Ebrington Barracks in Londonderry and my company received an invitation to attend the Londonderry Royal Military Police Cpl's Mess Christmas function.

I decided that I would take my good friend Cpl Steve Barratt (RIP) with me, along with his girlfriend and my wife. Steve had already done a tour in Northern Ireland and knew his way around. I had only been to Londonderry once, and that was in daylight. I knew Steve would therefore guide me up there.

So we loaded up my Ford Escort with the two girls and, for safety, drew two 9mm pistols from the armoury. These we stowed under the dashboard in the front of the car. We were not meant to use the Glenshane Pass, but we needed to get up to Londonderry in good time to enjoy ourselves. The journey was uneventful apart from when we drove through Dungiven.

It was not pub turning-out time, it was too early, but there were lots of people, both men and women, out on the streets. A local Christmas party was turning out. In any case, we were quickly surrounded by lots of drunken revellers and felt a bit threatened. They didn't know we were Security Forces, but that didn't matter. I saw Steve surreptitiously place his hands under the dashboard and cock one of the two 9mm pistols.

I drove very slowly, smiling and nodding to the people around us until we cleared the town centre and drove on. "What was that all about?" I asked. Steve just shook his head and said he had no idea, but it felt a bit hairy for a couple of minutes. When we drove back several hours later, the centre of Dungiven was empty and quiet and, with some relief, we drove home.

There was not much for Alison to do on her own for such long periods. We did use the Cpl's Mess as much as we could and were guests in the RAF Cpl's Mess as well. Fortunately, the Estate Manager for Aldergrove had been a friend of my dad's. He heard that Alison was a bit bored, so he asked her if she would consider helping in the newly built Married Quarters at Aldergrove. The houses had been completed, but before the Estate Manager moved all the furniture, beds, chairs, and so on in, the houses needed cleaning. So Alison, along with a couple of young lads from Crumlin, became a "Cleaning Crew". She found the work was good fun and the two young lads very chatty and friendly. The base at Aldergrove also had a cinema, which was well supported by all the forces personnel stationed there.

Dances in various Messes were a great attraction and lots of local girls used to make their way up to the barracks for these. The single men, of course, welcomed this. One of our young Lance Corporals, known

Chapter 15 - Upholding The Law

as "Titch," even went so far as to marry a local girl. I remember attending the church in Lisburn for the occasion. It didn't do him any harm as he ended up as a Regimental Sergeant Major (RSM).

Chippy (on the left) at the wedding of Doug
and Sue Smith at Killead Church

Another friend with whom I had shared a room in Berlin married one of the WRAC girls. They had their wedding at the small church in Killead, which backed onto the road where we lived. I was a member of his Guard of Honour and four of us in best "blues" and hats provided the "arch of truncheons" for Douggie and Sue to walk through on their way out of church.

An addition to this story is that at the time there were no vacant Married Quarters for Douggie and Sue to move into immediately.

So he parked a small caravan next to my mobile home and ran an extension lead into my place, to use the electricity. It was about this time that Alison and I went off to Hong Kong. I gave Douggie the house keys and the keys to my Ford Escort so he and Sue could be in relative comfort whilst we were away.

When I arrived back from Hong Kong, Douggie met us. He was looking sheepish, and I asked him what the matter was. He explained it was a problem with the car. When I asked him if he had crashed it, he replied, "No, but I filled it with diesel by mistake."

Luckily, our mechanical fitters and artificers came to the rescue. They emptied the petrol tank, flushed the system, and got it going again on petrol. It never did sound quite the same after that and it wasn't long before I sold the Escort and bought a Spitfire.

So, by the beginning of 1976 I had sold the Ford Escort that I brought from Germany and had bought a Triumph Spitfire coloured bright red. It was also left-hand drive and not exactly a low-profile car to be driving in Northern Ireland. Nevertheless, it was my pride and joy and after mucking up a total piston change, I had the whole engine rebuilt.

My off-duty time was spent totally with Alison. I had the occasional rugby match, but it was not easy travelling around the Province to play matches. Our mobile home was very small and the TV we had was a black and white portable that sat on a small coffee table in the living area of the mobile home. I tried to watch the TV news as much as possible to find out what was going on outside Northern Ireland. I can remember one incident that brought me to tears of frustration one evening. A news report came on of a bomb explosion somewhere in the Lower Falls. A Protestant man from the Shankill area drove over there with a load of chipboard on his vehicle and offered it to the locals to repair the damage. They accepted it gladly. He then went off to get a second load, and when he returned, he was shot dead by Republicans.

The report was about his funeral, which went from the Shankill over to the Lower Falls, where lots of people turned out to line the route of his cortege. I remember shouting at the TV with tears in my eyes, crying, "Why does it take tragedy to draw you bloody people together?" Out of all the incidents during the Troubles, that one will forever stick in my mind.

Samuel Llewellyn funeral, murdered because of his kindness

On February 12, 1976, I followed my orders and prepared to leave Northern Ireland with my wife Alison and our cat in my red Spitfire via the ferry from Belfast. It was a pleasant spring evening. The car was overloaded, including a cat box. That day, a Republican prisoner in England, Frank Stagg, died after going on a hunger strike that lasted 62 days. His death was immediately marked in the Republican areas of Belfast, and as my wife and I sat in the car on the dockside at Donegall Quay waiting to get on board, we distinctly heard a Tommy gun up in the Republican area of Belfast as it fired off a burst. There were several single shots in return, and it looked like the local Army units were in for a busy night. I was never so glad to get onto the Liverpool ferry. We were off to the HQ Allied Forces Central Europe (HQ AFCENT) at Brunssum in the Netherlands.

CHAPTER 16

Ten Years Later

Before I open this chapter, I should explain that after leaving Northern Ireland in 1976, I received several further postings. The first was to an international headquarters in the Netherlands for two years, followed by a posting to 156 Pro Coy in Colchester, Essex. In 1980, I was assigned to our training centre in Chichester, and from there to 111 Pro Coy in North Germany, where I served until 1984. Between my time in Colchester and Chichester, my wife and I sadly divorced. It would be in November 1984 that I was promoted to Sergeant (Sgt) and posted to 176 Pro Coy in Londonderry, Northern Ireland.

Unlike the first time I went to Northern Ireland in 1974, this time I was ahead of myself. I had properly registered my car with a Northern Ireland registration number before I even reached there. I managed this by contacting the AA, and they kindly did it all for me. Now feeling slightly more secure, I spent a day or two with Mum and Dad in Frimley, England, before starting off on the long and boring drive up to Liverpool.

As I was officially posted to Northern Ireland, the administration had already booked my ferry ticket from Liverpool to Belfast. This included a night in a hotel close to the docks where I was to board the boat.

The hotel that was allocated to me was a run-down establishment, standing on its own in a desolate wasteland of cleared houses. It stood out like a long tooth in the mouth of someone who had lost all their other teeth. The room was painted a dreary cream and brown colour with stains all over the walls, just to give it an edge. Then there was a long, thick chain, which was heavily bolted deep into the masonry wall, and wrapped around a small black-and-white television. Sometimes I do think that when the administration is booking hotels, when they see my name, they start from the bottom of their hotel list and not the top. I can say without any doubt or hesitation: what a dump.

Just to lift the atmosphere, I left the hotel, scouted the area, and found a chip shop. You might be thinking, *well, at least that was some comfort.* But they gave me a chip cone – where they take a real newspaper page, twist it into a cone shape, and drop the chips into it. And like an ice cream on a hot day melting through the bottom of its wafer cone, I could feel liquid running over my hand and dripping off in seconds. I think there was more grease in that cone than there were chips. I forced a few down my throat. It wasn't hard for them to slide down; the hard part was keeping them down. I went to bed that night with a stomach full of chip oil.

My stomach churned all night and the next morning I left the hotel and made my way in the car to the docks, then onto the ferry. Once again as I was travelling on duty, a cabin had been arranged for me, and I must admit I was glad to get into it – just to relax and consider that when I came off this boat, it would be a very different place than the part of the UK I had just left. Having been away from Northern Ireland for eight years, things had got nastier in my absence.

Before we were due to arrive in the harbour, I decided to go for some dinner and whether it was flashbacks or what, no matter who I saw in that restaurant, I thought I could see IRA terrorists in everyone's face and I was convinced everyone knew I was in the British Army. It

Chapter 16 - Ten Years Later

was now 1700 as I wandered through the restaurant over to the food counter. I selected a meal of some sort and approached the cashier and handed over my duty travel food voucher. I thought everything was going well until she said in a voice as Scouse as you could get and loud enough to be heard all over the ship, "If you're an Army lad son, you can have more than that if you want."

I could feel heat coming through my body, and it was like every eye in the place swung around to look at me, or some were already drawing knives from under their coats. I mumbled my thanks and walked towards the packed seating area, scanning for an empty seat.

Now what followed was one of those "sliding door" moments; turn left and find a seat or turn right? I turned right and caught a glimpse of an elderly gentleman and a young woman sitting at a table next to a window. The elderly gentleman had smart grey hair, and he had a pipe clenched in his teeth. The woman sitting opposite him was a lot younger, with shoulder-length jet-black hair, which she swept back with her left hand as she continued to write something in a book on the table. I caught a glimpse of ice-blue eyes, very pale clear white skin and a squarish face that was very pretty. I had a thing about women with long black hair, so I was glad I had turned right.

I made my way over to the table – which could seat six people – and asked if I might join them. The elderly gentleman said I could, so I took a seat and tucked into my food, glancing every now and then at the young woman and the man. The gentleman then stood up and asked to be excused as he was going outside to smoke his pipe. With his departure I paid even more attention to the young woman, who continued reading her textbook and making notes in another book.

I plucked up some courage and asked, "Are you a teacher?" She gave a slight sigh of exasperation and said, "I hope to be shortly. I am studying for my PGCE" (Postgraduate Certificate in Education).

I replied, "Oh, so you already have a degree?" I ventured. She said, "Well yes, two in fact. I have just finished my PhD in Birmingham and am on my way home to Belfast with my father."

A PhD! That means she's a doctor. Smart and stunning – clearly, I was out of my depth. "I'd like to be a teacher one day too," I added, pretending I had my life as together as she clearly did.

"Oh, really," she countered, "best of luck," and went back to her reading and writing. Just then the elderly gentleman returned, and I struck up a conversation with him. He said he lived in Belfast, and as I had to drive to Derry/Londonderry that evening, I asked if he could give me directions out of Belfast and onto the Londonderry Road. Well, that got the conversation going and I managed to introduce myself. I was still wary of who these two were and of course most important in Northern Ireland, where they lived. The gentleman replied that he was Billy Farris, and introduced me officially to his daughter, who was called Alison Farris. Finding out their names, I thought, they are good Protestant names, at least they shouldn't be out to kill me. At least we are off to a good start.

For those of you who are not familiar with the way things happen with the locals in Northern Ireland, let me give you an example. If you joined a bus queue, within a few minutes, the people in the queue will know all about you, your family, where you went to school etc. They do this painlessly and you hardly realise it is happening.

During the Troubles, the people never would travel outside their area far and in doing so, a stranger entering their area was easily recognised, making them a terrorist, or undercover soldier, but likely not a tourist, as travellers were nervous of visiting Northern Ireland in those days. But they sure do make up for it today in tourism terms.

Family names have a strong link to religion in Northern Ireland. For example, if Billy had said his name was "Seamus" and that Alison was

Chapter 16 - Ten Years Later

"Fionnuala" or something similar, I would have guessed they were both Roman Catholics and I would have been very wary of telling them anything about myself. The same goes for where you live in Belfast. The Falls Road is dodgy Republican, but the Shankill is safer for soldiers, as it's Loyalist. Initially the soldiers were brought in to protect the Catholics and the Catholic mothers would make tea and sandwiches for them. That changed quickly, and tea and sandwiches were soon swapped for petrol bombs and rocks.

Billy, although elderly, still had his wits about him and from my accent it did not take him long to figure out that I was in the military. He admitted to having served in the RAF during the war, so immediately we had common ground and I felt more at ease. Alison ignored this conversation of course; she was still head down in her books. By the time we docked, I had managed to ask Billy if I might call in on him and his family if I were ever in Belfast and to that end could I ask for his telephone number? He gave it readily and I made my farewells.

* * *

Oh, how Belfast had changed since the last time I served there. I had been travelling in my car on the way to Derry/Londonderry and I got onto the M2 motorway, only to find it ran out just outside of Toome. This village was known for being Republican and the RUC Station there was heavily fortified due to the attacks it had received. It was an eerie feeling driving through Toome in the wee small hours of the morning. For if the army were not lying in the hedges ready to jump out in a split second to stop a vehicle, the IRA was never far away. As I drove over Toome Bridge heading north, I checked my mirrors and the road behind me was dark, so at least I wasn't being followed.

Driving past Magherafelt I was aware that South Londonderry was a very sectarian county. You would need to have been raised in that area to understand what to say or not to say, even what to wear, and even which shops to give your money to. Some people would walk to the other side of the town just to spend their money with people of the same religion as themselves and the shop owner.

I became friendly with one of the soldiers – we'll call him Gusty – from Magherafelt. One day we were chatting about me being raised in England and what it was like. Then he explained, "I don't think you understand the depth of religious hatred there is here. We could be united in playing after-school football on the street or in a playground. Even playing football just for a bit of fun, if a Catholic tackled a Protestant harshly, immediately all the Protestants would face off with the Catholics. Religion was always the deciding factor."

Gusty continued, "I remember a day when ten of us were spending time together, about seven of us were Protestants and three were Catholics and as we stood in Magherafelt on Queen Street, also known as the Moneymore Pass, we noticed a Chinese family. They were walking along the pavement on the other side of the road. There was a mother, father, and a few children who were around my age – at High School – and some were younger.

For the next few minutes, we were mesmerised; we had never seen a Chinese person in real life, and in fact the only person we knew of who looked like them was Bruce Lee, and as he was Chinese, so they must be too.

A couple of the boys crossed over the road and followed them into a shop. Somehow or other, the oldest girl was trailing behind the family and one of our bolder boys asked her, "Are you a Catholic or Protestant Chinese?"

The girl just shrugged her shoulders. Maybe she didn't understand our accents or didn't speak English. We had our own in-house discussion among ourselves, trying to decide whether they were Catholic or Protestant Chinese.

Chapter 16 - Ten Years Later

We decided we would wait to see what school they would go to: if they went to a Catholic school, then they were Catholics; if they went to a Protestant school, then they were Protestants."

At this point I had fallen into the trap and asked, "What school did they go to?" Gusty laughed and said, "The Rainey – a grammar that takes both!"

By now I was on the Glenshane Pass and, as anyone who has travelled that long hill back then would recall, the car engine started to struggle. The car was slowing down by itself, until I was in second gear.

With the car being so slow, I remembered Gusty sharing about the Glenshane Pass, and that the area was a training ground for the IRA. Before I realised it, my eyes were scanning the dark moss mountain on the left, wondering whether I would see even a glimpse from flashlamp or suchlike. That night there was nothing to see. The car engine came back to life as we reached the top of the hill and off I went as the sun began to rise. The valley became full of mist, and there was not another car on the road. I had the radio on when the theme from "Harry's Game" by Clannad came on. I will never forget those small moments when the music and the scenery made such an impression on me. Soon I would arrive at Clooney Base in Londonderry.

The base had once been an American communications centre, located on the south side of the River Foyle, the same side as Ebrington Barracks and a Republican area known as Gobnascale. Free Derry corner, the Bogside and the Creggan were all over the river on the other side from Clooney.

I was surprised to find, when I walked into the Duty Room, both the Regimental Sergeant Major (RSM)[33] and the Officer Commanding (OC) were present. There was a smell of cordite in the air, and I quickly became aware that something had happened.

---

[33] Regimental Sergeant Major is responsible for all aspects of discipline of the warrant officers, NCOs, and men and is, or should be, the Colonel"s confidant.

It turned out that a Corporal who was attached to the Special Investigation Branch (SIB) of the Royal Military Police had accidentally discharged his pistol in the Duty Room. The gun smoke was still visible, floating about seven feet up in the air.

The Regimental Sergeant Major told me that a bunk had been arranged for me in the Sergeant's Mess and it was best if I went straight to bed and reported to him in the morning.

The next morning, I discovered that the Second in Command of 176 Provost Company Royal Military Police was my old boss from my time at the Training Centre in Chichester whom I had served with before in England. We were pleased to see each other, and he congratulated me on my promotion. I reported to the Regimental Sergeant Major and received a not-very-friendly welcome speech from this person whom I had known in Berlin when he was the Assistant Provost Marshal's clerk.[34] He still talked and acted like a clerk as well. I was told that I would be kitted out with what I required and that the first thing I had to do was to attend a Northern Ireland Reinforcement Training Team (NIRTT) at Ballykinler army camp near Newcastle, County Down.

This was completely different from my first tour where if you recall I was just thrown in at the deep end. This time I had to go off for a week's course on how to move about like an infantryman, conduct vehicle and people checks, and get up to speed on the current Northern Ireland situation. I was told to take my car and take a 9mm pistol and a 7.62mm Self Loading Rifle (SLR) with me in the boot.

I made my way down to Ballykinler as ordered. As a new Senior Non-Commissioned Officer, I was put in charge of a mixed section of men from all corps and regiments of the British Army. We were taught about moving into built-up areas, doing spot checks on suspects, and being brought up to date on the latest legislation regarding the detention of terrorist suspects.

---

[34] Provost Marshal"s clerk advises on all issues related to: Force Protection, Law Enforcement, Anti-terrorism, Physical Security and Domestic Threats.

One of the main "training aids" at Ballykinler was the "Tin City". This was a mock-up of several streets in a built-up area with houses, shops, a church, etc. and in addition, there were vehicles parked in various places. Now all these vehicles were "wired up" so that at any time when you could be passing them, they would suddenly "start up" and make engine noises. There were also strategically placed mannequins, up alleyways for instance who, as you passed them, would turn round and "fire" at you. This resulted in "contact drills" and what to do if you did come under fire. It was all good training. I was in charge of one such "foot" patrol when we came under fire from an alleyway. We returned fire, using blank ammunition of course, but the gunman, as in the mannequin, kept firing.

34 Ballykinler "Tin City" training camp

It was near lunchtime and one of the patrols was hungry. As he ran up the alleyway, shooting at this dummy, jumping on top of it, sending it to the ground and then smashing it with his rifle butt. He was teaching these plastic gunmen not to mess with him, especially when he was hungry.

The instructor gave him praise for "reaction to enemy fire" but told him that one-man suicide charges are not the way to go about things. The end of the week culminated in getting into and out of helicopters because it was highly likely we would end up being taken in one at some point. It was a free trip around the bay in the helicopter that ended the week of training.

In an earlier part of my service, I was in the Depot and Training Establishment of the Royal Military Police in Chichester when two Junior Non-Commissioned Officers, after having had too many beers one evening, decided to try to hitch a ride to Aldershot to see a girlfriend. During this journey, they kidnapped the driver of a car and stole his car to get to Aldershot. The result of this was that both were court-martialled and discharged from the Royal Military Police. One of them was a Corporal, known as Clive, who, when sober, was a first-class bloke. He was a Physical Training Instructor and a great all-round sportsman. He had had to go home to his parents after being dismissed from the Corps. His Father was a Warrant Officer Class 1, which is the highest non-commissioned rank and Regimental Sergeant Major in the Special Investigation Branch (SIB), which was the detective branch of the Royal Military Police.

Clive was living in Ballykinler and could not find much to do in the way of work in Northern Ireland as an ex-soldier and just to keep himself busy he had taken up a job as a lifeguard in the military swimming pool within the Camp.

One day, he was noticed by the Commanding Officer of the resident regiment, the Devon and Dorset Regiment (D&D) who asked him to tell his story. Clive did just that, and the Commanding Officer was magnanimous enough to offer him employment back in the Army with a clean slate, provided he joined the Devon and Dorset Regiment. The Commanding Officer had the power to do this and obviously recognised that Clive would make a good soldier if he was given another chance. With the Devon and Dorset Regiment being the resident Regiment, Clive naturally opted to join them.

He rose quickly through the ranks and when I went to Ballykinler was already a Lance Corporal. I made a point of finding him to have a chat, but he was very reticent and a bit embarrassed by his past. I left him to it, but I was to bump into him again only a month or two later.

At the end of the Ballykinler training, I had to make my way back to Londonderry. But before I would return, I decided to take advantage of the fact that I still had Billy's telephone number, and I made the call to ask if I could visit and see him. Now, I know what you are thinking: yes, of course it was Alison I wanted to see, but that was too obvious and not the way to do things.

So, I telephoned and had a good five-minute chat with Billy and then asked, "Was Alison about?" I held my breath, wondering if the answer would be "No", or "She is busy" – in other words, she didn't want to speak with me.

"Hold on," Billy said, I hadn't thought of "hold on" as a reply, and somehow, whether it was nerves or what, I held my breath.

When I heard the phone being sat down, I took a breath. Billy had gone to Alison and told her I was on the telephone, wanting to speak to her.

You would have thought she would have been excited, but no, she asked, "What did I want to speak to her about?" I explained that I had finished my training at Ballykinler and was not needed back in Londonderry base until Sunday night. Would she consider letting me take her out for the evening?

The result was that I set off to Belfast for the evening. I was not expected back in Londonderry until Monday. I had civilian clothes with me, so I could go out into Belfast if that was the choice. The good news is, she said, "Yes."

When I arrived at Alison's house in Belfast, a problem arose. I still had the 9mm pistol and the SLR in the boot. I explained this to Billy, and he said it would be best if I put them behind the door in the downstairs cloakroom. He was happy enough with this suggestion and I placed them there. I changed into my civvy clothes and Alison was beautifully dressed.

For me, rust had set into my dating ideas, and I asked her what she would like to do. She mentioned the Lyric Theatre and as I liked the theatre and had not been to one for a long time, we decided to go there.

We watched "*Can't pay? Won't pay!*" and then opted to go to a Chinese restaurant in Donegall Pass. As we were queued waiting inside the restaurant for a table, a typical Belfast man commented how good we looked like a couple. I replied that this was our first date, so we were still finding our feet. He then announced this to the whole restaurant, and we got winks and smiles. Such a thing would only happen in Belfast!

During dinner, I had worked out that Alison was a remarkable academic scientist, "brains to burn" as they would say in Northern Ireland. Yet, she had been very unlucky when it came to affairs of the heart.

After dinner, we called it an early night and on getting back to Alison's house, I played the "it's-too-late-to-drive-back-to-Derry-I-shall-have-to-stay-the-night" card. That was not a problem, so after a Bushmills nightcap, Alison gave me enough bedding to make a bed up on the front-room floor. I slept well that night with a smile on my face, except for a cuckoo that felt the need to say hello to me every hour and a half. All I can say is that cuckoo clock was lucky it was not mine.

Chapter 16 - Ten Years Later

The next morning, after breakfast, I made my way back to Londonderry, ready to start work with my new platoon and section.

The working system in Londonderry was based on a rota. It consisted of four weeks manning a border checkpoint with the infantry based in County Fermanagh, followed by two week's leave. On returning to work, it became two weeks of mobile and foot patrols around the Waterside and Gobnascale areas of Londonderry, followed by four weeks of manning the three checkpoints on the approaches to Londonderry: Muff, Moville, and Letterkenny.

These last three places were on the north side of the River Foyle and getting to them sometimes was a bit hazardous. It was so dangerous because there was just one road from the city out to the Letterkenny Checkpoint and it would be very easy to ambush us on our way. At times when it was seen as too dangerous to drive because of the threat, we flew by helicopter from Clooney to the checkpoints and it was only a three-mile journey. The platoon I joined was about to begin the four-week Fermanagh section of duties, and I was sent to man the road checkpoint at Rosslea on the Fermanagh/Monaghan border. This meant that we were picked up by Wessex helicopter from Clooney base, then flown to Lisnaskea where we got a second helicopter, a Lynx, which dropped us off in a field beside the checkpoint.

The checkpoint itself was a breeze-block compound in which there were four portacabins, two for sleeping in, one for a bathroom and one was the kitchen. There was a short tower on one wall of the compound that was located by the side of the main road. The tower had a radio and an all-observation kit at the bottom of it, and up a ladder was a small room with a General-Purpose Machine Gun (GPMG) and searchlight in it. We also had illumination rockets and a 40mm Grenade launcher. The road was controlled by traffic lights at the north end and south end by the men in the tower. That way, we could check one car at a time as it came through the checkpoint.

Rosslea PVCP

The border was another half mile down the road. The "white" gatepost on the right has a small metal box and inside it was a ***"Stinger"*** [35]

---

[35] A spike strip is a device used to stop wheeled vehicles by puncturing their tyres.

Chapter 16 - Ten Years Later

The shift pattern was four hours on and eight hours off. That lasted for four weeks. We were resupplied by road or helicopter, depending on the security situation. I was part of a team of three: myself and two corporals. The idea was that Military Police were better trained at asking questions of passing motorists rather than infantrymen, who were generally less interested.

About a week into the four-week stint, a message arrived asking for one of my team, otherwise known as Tiny, to proceed to Lisburn, where he was required to represent the Army Northern Ireland in a rugby match against the Public-School Wanderers. I felt a bit put out. I was still classed as a new boy in the Province, so no one knew that I was a decent rugby player.

We were inside the sleeping accommodation when Corporal Carroll, who was ironing his uniform, suddenly gasped in pain and stated that he had pulled his back and could hardly stand up. I'm sure we all put ourselves forward at some points, so please don't judge. As quickly as I could, ignoring Cpl Carroll's discomfort, I telephoned the selectors and told them I was a last-minute replacement. A few days later, I was airlifted out to go and train with the rest of the team in Omagh. I quickly contacted Alison and told her that if she wanted to see me, I would be playing rugby in Thiepval Barracks in Lisburn on 6 December 1984.

On the day in question, Alison came to watch, and it was a freezing afternoon. The team we played was all current or ex-internationals and there were some famous names in there. I won't give our team list because it was just fifteen military lads. However, there was one name, apart from mine, that stood out on the Army team list. Lance Corporal Clive from the Devon and Dorset Regiment (D&D). I told you he would pop up again.

Now, if you know about local rugby, that was some team. We did our best, and when you have your girl on the sideline and seeking to impress her, one gives that extra boost during the playtime. Although I don't think about how many boosts I or my team would give, if memory serves me well, we lost 20–10.

The whistle blew, the game was over, and I staggered over to Alison, who I could see was trembling with cold on the touchline. Like most men, I just wanted her to say, "You played well" or such like. But she tried to smile at me, with her lips and teeth shaking, and asked, "Who won?"

I was aghast! I could not believe that I had fallen for a girl who knew absolutely nothing about rugby. Was she not aware rugby was my first love? I am glad to say that she saved the situation very well by producing a bottle of Powers whisky from her coat pocket and offering it to me to warm up. She went right up in my estimation and unknowingly challenged my first love head-on.

CHAPTER 17

The British Ambassador – Not

I was invited to visit some friends in America, acquaintances that I met in Germany when I served there.

I booked my flight with British Airways and made my way to Heathrow after catching the shuttle from Belfast to London. At the check-in, there was a long queue waiting. Suddenly, the ticket agent on the desk announced that the desk was now closed, and we would all have to go around to "Late Bookings." I spoke to the ticket agent and pointed out that two desks had been used to book our flight, but these were now closed and we were directed to a single desk. It did not make sense.

I did manage to get booked onto the flight, but was told there was no guarantee my luggage would be on board the aircraft, as it was under "Late Bookings." This was, of course, a cause for concern as I had packed my brand-new sergeant's mess kit uniform just in case there would be an opportunity to wear it.

The aircraft was a Boeing 747, which flew from London to Ottawa. Then I had the whole plane to myself for the last leg of the journey, to Detroit. The stewardess kept me supplied with food, and after I explained my lack of baggage, she informed me I could claim an overnight bag from BA. The first opportunity I had, I claimed it. It consisted of enough items to allow me to keep going for a day or two.

I landed in Detroit and was met by one of my friends driving a Ford Mustang. It was early evening, so once we got back to their parent's home, I met her father, who was Polish/American and worked for Ford in Detroit. In the back garden of their home was a dismantled amphibious aircraft! I thought, does every American home have one? The father was a nice man and proudly showed me his .30 Carbine that he had kept after the war. It had been modified to fire a single shot rather than being automatic. I knew most American homes had a gun, but with him having a daughter, was he warning me against messing about with her, or just letting me know he had a weapon?

On December 22, we went to the Pontiac Silverdome, where I watched the University of Michigan play the Army team, which, of course, was West Point Military Academy rather than the regular Army. It was quite a show and lasted for over three hours.

Christmas Day arrived, and in the USA, it is just like any other day. The shops were all open, and you would not know it was a holiday. Plus, it was freezing cold and yet bright and sunny.

After lunch, I went to take a walk outside and nearly froze to death after fifty yards. It was something like 20 below!

Then on Boxing Day, we had planned a trip and off we went in the Mustang to Frankenmuth, a town founded by Lutheran settlers on the shores of Lake Michigan. There we drank "steins" of German beer, ate typical Bavarian food and then drove home stuffed to the gills. I did not realise that food portions in America are meant to kill you in one go.

It was there that I got introduced to a police officer, one of Detroit's finest. He was Irish/American and a bit wary of me when he heard I was a British Soldier.

Chapter 17 - The British Ambassador–Not

Nevertheless, he invited me to go out on patrol one night with him and another officer. They showed me around all the good parts of Detroit, where Aretha Franklin's father had been shot, and where the riots had taken place. I thought, "I can get enough of this in Northern Ireland". They were tasked with a report of someone trespassing in a factory block and off we went. The officer let me out of the back of the Police cruiser – the doors could only be opened from the outside – and then asked me if I knew how to handle a shotgun. I replied I did, whereupon one was produced from the boot of the cruiser, and I was asked to stand guard on the car whilst they went off and investigated. I was left by the police car in possession of a Remington pump-action 12-bore. I began to wonder what would happen if we came under gunfire and another police car turned up to find a strange man in civilian clothes standing next to a police car with a shotgun in his hands. Fortunately, they came back after about ten minutes and reported that all was quiet.

After we finished about midnight, I was invited to his home, which had a cellar bar. The place was decked out in all things Irish: flags, pictures, leprechauns, and so on. I noticed a map of Ireland on the wall, and I pointed out that it was not an up-to-date one, and asked, "Is this an old map, as it does not have the Northern Ireland/Ireland border on it?" He explained in his own little way that Ireland was one country, and as soon as the invading British Army left, the Irish would be fine.

I then gently informed him of the Protestant part of Northern Ireland, those who considered themselves British, and I was amazed that he was under the impression that England had "invaded" Ireland only a few years before. I thought to myself, "This is how NORAID gets its funding."

On the final night of my stay, it was arranged for us to go to the Joe Louis Centre for dinner. I was excited, as this was my chance to dress up and put on my dress kit, as my baggage had arrived three days earlier. One of the guys had a friend who rented out and drove stretched limousines. Now this was on the cards; with an opportunity not to be missed, we decided then to cruise around in the limo.

Detroit Xmas 1984
Posing for a photo in the cellar bar of Lori-Annes,
with a friend who was the limo driver/owner

At one point, we were cruising alongside a car packed with four black lads who kept staring at our flashy limo. I wound down the rear window and called out to them, "Happy Christmas, gentlemen!"

"Hey!" one of them yelled back, "look, it's the British Ambassador!"

Bloody hell, I thought, a military uniform really works magic over here.

Inside the massive restaurant at the Joe Louis Centre, we were escorted to our table like VIPs. My dress uniform caused quite a stir – one woman actually gasped, "Oh my God, look at him!"

"Careful, madam," I shot back with a grin, "the redcoats are coming!"

That brought the house down.

Despite all this American razzmatazz, I was itching to get back home to Alison and catch up on how she was getting on with her PGCE at Queen's University Belfast. The Londonderry duty rota was waiting, my Open University studies were heating up in my second year, and before long I'd be heading back to Fermanagh – Rosslea, here I come again.

CHAPTER 18

We Only Have to Be Lucky Once

Just before we deployed south again, it was decided to have a day on the ranges. Strangely, there was a small 25m range just off the main Londonderry – Limavady Road. We decided to use that.

It was just a small area fenced in with a very high chain-link fence and secured by a padlocked main gate. At the firing point of the range was a set of pits dug into the soil to be used as cover when firing. We decided they looked too wet and cold, so we just did our practice from the standing and kneeling position. It was just as well we did, because the platoon that followed us a week later was a bit more switched on and decided to use the pits. As the first one was opened, a booby-trap bomb was found inside that had failed to detonate. Perhaps it was meant for us the week before, but one never knows.

Having had our day on the ranges, the authorities decided that, to take full advantage of our training time, we would return to the ranges, but this time to the proper ranges inside Ballykelly Barracks (now City of Derry Airport.)

We duly turned up and spent a fruitful day firing off goodness knows how much money's worth of pyrotechnics down the range. We fired the SLR, the 9mm pistol and of course the SMG. At this point, as a Senior Non-Commissioned Officer, I was asked to take command of a group of six Junior Non-Commissioned Officers as they underwent an SMG shooting exercise. It all went well until one Junior Non-Commissioned Officer put his hand up to say he had a live round stuck in the breech of his SMG. This did happen from time to time as the charge inside a particular round was not producing as much of an explosive effect as it should, and this resulted in the working parts, i.e. the bolt and breech, not extracting the empty round before firing the next one. In this case, the round had not gone off and was half in and half out of the barrel. The reason for this issue was likely that we had been using a lot of ammunition that came from India. The turnover of ammunition in Northern Ireland was causing shortages, and this "Indian" ammunition was a bit dodgy. Whereas we were used to taking shiny, new brass-encased rounds from a box, much of this ammunition was slightly discoloured by heat and dampness.

The proper procedure was to unload the weapon, place it down and get the armourer to sort it out. However, a young officer stepped forward and said to the Junior Non-Commissioned Officer holding the weapon, "It's OK. Just fire off the gun as usual and the weight of the bolt will ram it up the barrel and it will go off, OK?" The Junior Non-Commissioned Officer did as he was told and immediately a breech explosion occurred, which blew the bolt back into the body of the weapon while at the same time ejecting hot gases and bits of brass and lead out the side of the weapon and into the firer's face!

I immediately shouted to all the others on the firing point to "Unload!" and lay down their weapons. First Aid was required as the firer had small wounds to his face that required attention. Fortunately, his eyes were okay. Unfortunately, the weapon had to be seized as evidence and the young officer had to appear before a Unit Enquiry to explain why he had given such a stupid order when he was not in charge, and why he had deviated from safe practice. He got what was called "an interview without coffee" with the Brigade Commander.

Chapter 18 - We Only Have to Be Lucky Once

RMP in the Loading & Unloading Bay. Nearest the camera is an RAFP[36]

So off I went once again to do a four-week stint at Rosslea on the Fermanagh/Monaghan border. This time I had my camera with me. It was early March as I distinctly remember doing duty on the checkpoint road in the snow. I also recall being "on the road" on St Patrick's Day as well, so that places me there on March 17, 1985.

After several days, an undercover, non-uniformed 14 Int man – let's call him Soldier A for now – asked me if the person he was interested in had driven through the checkpoint yet. I told him he had not. He then asked me to go back out onto the road and, when the person concerned drove up from the border, to let him know. An hour or so later, Soldier A appeared dressed in uniform and asked me to swap berets with him, allowing him to take my place on the road.

---

[36] RAFP - Royal Air Force Police.

We had been informed that the man he wanted to question was en route to us, unaware that the soldier waiting to stop him was from 14 Intelligence Company. Trained by the SAS, these men had extensive experience in undercover surveillance against suspected members of terrorist groups.

By this time, I had moved to the side of the checkpoint, and it wasn't long before the car we had been waiting for was now in our eyesight. Once the driver had reached Soldier A, he directed the driver to drive his car into our secure compound. Then, as if Soldier A had known the driver all his life, he followed the car inside and jumped in beside him. That became a long chat. In the meantime, I had gone back onto the road, still wearing a black beret.

Once all the cloak-and-dagger action was over, we waited until there were no other vehicles in sight, then directed the man out of the compound and he drove off back into the Republic. Soldier A did tell me that he had had a good talk with the man; he would give him money to pay for his road tax and insurance, plus a bit more besides, in return for letting let the Security Forces know when and if anything "exciting" was about to happen.

I never found out whether my stint at Rosslea had produced results as this would be my last duty there. What I did know was that 14 Intelligence Company were absolutely brilliant at their job. They'd successfully recruited informers right throughout the republican movement – penetrating straight to the top of Sinn Féin's leadership.

It reinforced something important: there was real value in actually chatting with people instead of just waving them through to keep the queue moving. You never knew what might come up in conversation.

During a snowy spell, I was "on the road" checking passing cars when the soldier in the tower called down that a foot patrol was approaching

Chapter 18 - We Only Have to Be Lucky Once

from the Rosslea side of the checkpoint. When they came in, it turned out to be a joint RUC/British Army foot patrol out patrolling the countryside. We let them in, of course, and put the kettle on as anyone with guests would do. The senior RUC Constable then produced a plastic bottle from his rucksack and proceeded to put a good shot of a clear watery liquid into our large teacups.

"What's this?" I asked, "Don't worry" he replied, "just put a spoonful of sugar in there and top it up with hot water."

I did and took a careful sip of a sweet, fiery liquid that warmed me up from my toes to my head. "What is it? I asked.

"Poteen," he replied, "we knocked over an illegal still last night, so we all have a bottle or two to ward off the cold!"

It was a nice change to have a sip or two, as in certain areas, especially along the border, we relied on helicopter supply runs for our rations. In those days, there was no such thing as home delivery. And even if there had been, I doubt anyone would've volunteered to bring it into such a targeted zone.

With nine soldiers living in, sleeping in, and running the vehicle checkpoints (VCPs), food had a way of vanishing into someone's belly, leaving the rest of us short of essentials. Chief among them was eggs.

One of those days arrived when several of us fancied an egg, but there were none to be found. Thanks to our surveillance equipment and reports from 14 Intelligence Company, I knew that just south of the checkpoint, between us and the Irish border in a sort of no-man's land, sat a chicken farm. Unfortunately, it belonged to a family who, let's just say, weren't exactly keen on helping the British Army. Some of them were Sinn Féin members, and God only knew what else.

Whenever any of the family's sons drove through our checkpoint, he'd get a cocky smirk and the sneering question: "How's it going, soldier boy?" Then followed quickly, "Have you caught the mad bomber yet?"

What they didn't know was that it would be their very own farm helping to keep us fed. So you've got to ask – who had the last smirk?

Lo and behold, you wouldn't believe it. The very day I could practically taste that egg on toast, even though we had none, I started wondering if God had sent an angel. All I can say is, we were about to find out.

Here he comes, I whispered to myself. It was the son's father coming through the checkpoint and – are you ready for this? – he was by himself. This gave me the advantage, as no one else would overhear our conversation. I put on my friendliest smile and asked, "How are you today, John?" (I'll call him John for now). You see, we were trained in memorising faces and names, car number plates and so forth. The idea was always to let those who opposed you know that we knew exactly who they were.

He was in a friendly mood and asked how the day was going and so forth. It was then that I leaned into the car window and asked, "Would you sell us some eggs? We've run out."

Knowing this could be the very person who might help plan an attack against us, those few seconds waiting for his answer felt like forever. He looked me straight in the eye and... as I waited for the "Yes" or "No", neither came. Instead, he said, "I'll be back in a few minutes," and drove off. Honestly, I didn't know what had happened – were we getting eggs or not?

About thirty minutes passed and I was still at the checkpoint, focusing on who was driving through and why, when the sangar guard shouted at me, "The egg man is back!" He'd spotted the car in the distance.

Chapter 18 - We Only Have to Be Lucky Once

Other checkpoints were equipped with what was known as *Op Vengeful*,[37] a number-plate scanner that flagged vehicles linked to suspected terrorist families as they came through the line. Unfortunately, we did not have one, so the alert came in the old way – by a raised voice.

When his turn came to drive forward to where I was stationed, I looked north and south to make sure there were no other vehicles around and told the soldier in the sangar to change the traffic light to "green." John drove as calmly as you like. He nodded with his finger – a "Hello" or, as they say in Northern Ireland, "What bout ye?"

He wound down the window, reached over to the passenger seat and handed me a tray of twenty-four large, fresh eggs.

I thought I'd won the lottery. I couldn't wait to smell those fresh eggs cooking. "Thank you, sir," I said, and asked, "How much will that be? We've had a whip-round and I can pay you."

"No," he replied, "take them please, but whatever you do, don't tell the family."

This was Northern Ireland in a nutshell – the same family that bred Republican militants also bred a man willing to risk his life, giving eggs to British troops, knowing others had been shot for much less.

As I went to crack the eggshell to fry my egg, a thought suddenly hit me: "Were these eggs given to us by a friend or the enemy?" If a friend, all good. If the enemy, could he have injected something into them? Oh well, I can only die once, so let's do it with an egg in my mouth.

---

[37] *Op Vengeful* was used to identify vehicles linked to subjects of interest, with checks coordinated through the Driver and Vehicle Licensing Agency (DVLA) of Northern Ireland. Vehicle Registration Numbers (VRNs) associated to these individuals were recorded on a card index system, maintained by Intelligence Sections across the Province. Those manning Vehicle Checkpoints (VCPs) would then be briefed on what checks to carry out on the driver, passengers, and vehicle.

The system predated computers – hence the reliance on landline calls to the DVLA – and remained in use from 1971 until 1980, when local databases finally replaced the old phone-and-paper method.

I can say I lived to write this book and, what's more, it wasn't the last batch that John would deliver... but do remember – don't tell his family.

***

When on leave, I would spend most of my time with Alison in Belfast, and at weekends she would catch the train from Belfast to Londonderry to visit me.

I can never forget that first time when she came to visit me in Londonderry. I got myself all cleaned up, and you could likely have sniffed the aftershave off me a mile away, with the amount of it I had splashed on. I had already pinpointed a place where I could purchase fresh flowers en route to the train station and that day, I chose the nicest bunch of yellow roses they had, got them wrapped and continued my journey. Did I forget to say, I had a hip flask of whisky in my pocket for nerves.

I don't know about you, but as you have learnt, I have been in bombings, shootings, lying in hedges and so forth, not needing a flask of whisky in my pocket – and yet here I was, nerves beating like the 12th of July, all over a woman.

There she was, wrapped in a warm jacket as it was one of those blustery Northern Ireland weekends, her long black hair blowing in the breeze, which she pushed back over her head so she could see what she was doing. This revealed her fair round face and deep blue eyes. She had a smile on her face and as we came together, we had a firm hug and I gave her a peck on the lips; you see, I never was one for snogging in public. The fact that she had come all the way up from Belfast to spend the weekend with me was a great sign. She knew that I lived in the Mess and that there were two single beds in my room, but I had placed them together months earlier, secured them with belts and bungees and managed to get an extra mattress and double sheets! I believed in comfort.

I gave Alison the bunch of yellow roses that I had bought for her and told her my hip flask was full of whisky and in my pocket. She smiled a sort of knowing smile, the hidden meaning of which I did not realise at the time. She asked if we could drive up towards Magilligan, as she had a soil erosion project to complete for her PGCE and she wanted to photograph the sand dunes there.

That very day at the beach – Alison at Magilligan 1985

Alison's visit was about more than just seeing me; she was in fact, coming to tell me that she wanted to end our relationship. She would later admit to having been in a string of disastrous relationships and did not want to get "involved" again at such short notice. She initially had confided this to a friend called Yvonne, who suggested that Alison should "give him the elbow, give him the push." Being the person she is, Alison did not want to do this over the telephone, so had come all the way to tell me herself. Me turning up with roses and a flask of whisky changed her mind, and the rest, as they say, is history. She didn't tell me this straight away; it was a few weeks later when we were in Belfast together and out for the night in the city centre. Never before had a bunch of roses and a flask of whisky been so important! If ever I am in the doghouse now, I bring home yellow roses.

I was on my second tour down in Fermanagh when Alison, who had successfully completed her PGCE, applied for a biology teaching post at an all-girls private school in Potters Bar, just on the outskirts of north London. She rang me from Liverpool Street railway station whilst I was in the compound at Rosslea, to tell me she had got the job. On a poor line I asked what we were going to do next. She replied that she did not know.

I said, "Well, it looks like you will have to marry me then." Her reply was, "I can see my train standing at the platform, I will have to go." With that, she dropped the phone and ran!

Between then and when we finally left Northern Ireland, life turned out to be anything but quiet and cosy.

I applied to the Hertfordshire Constabulary to join the force and of course, there was a lot of paperwork and checks to be done on me. I had to sit a written exam, the only place being the RUC Station at Strand Road, Londonderry. I turned up at the appointed hour, having been dropped off by one of the patrols. I entered the classroom where the exam was to take place and saw that there were about a dozen other hopefuls, all dressed in civilian clothes, as they were all locals.

The other candidates must have wondered if this guy was going to war or sitting an exam, or what was going on, as I had to strip off helmet, flak jacket, combat jacket and weapon before I could even sit down.

I was invited to Hertfordshire and the night before I flew from Belfast to London, Alison and I had been to see "*A Passage to India*" at the cinema. Dave Allen, the comedian, was performing in the theatre next door. As I boarded the aircraft, I noticed Rev. Ian Paisley behind me – the firebrand Loyalist politician and churchman.

I thought, "That's it, this plane is doomed." Then, just after I sat down, who else should join the aircraft but Dave Allen? I immediately thought, "Ah, well, we are okay now. The devil looks after his own."

Of course, we arrived safely in London – otherwise you wouldn't be reading this book. At the luggage carousel, I found myself standing right next to Dave Allen. I struck up a conversation and told him that the previous evening we had had a choice between seeing his show or "*A Passage to India*".

"Which did you choose?" he wondered. I replied, "*The Passage to India*." "Good choice," he said with a grin. Then he asked what I was doing in Northern Ireland, and when I told him I was in the military based in Londonderry, he exclaimed, "Jesus, even I wouldn't do a show in Derry!"

After that, I travelled to Welwyn Garden City for my Hertfordshire Constabulary interview at Headquarters. I completed the physical tests, written exams, and interviews. Once everything was completed, I was told I had passed and, if it suited me, I could join the force in early 1986. That was perfect. It gave me enough time to give proper notice to the Army and the Royal Military Police, so they could arrange a replacement and get me back to England.

Our role in Londonderry, as I've said, was less about policing and more about playing poorly trained infantry. To be clear, we were not infantry, but for command purposes we fell under the local battalion. The result? Highly trained military policemen walking the streets of the Waterside area of Londonderry, acting as though they were basic infantrymen.

Our standard weapon was the 9mm SMG, sometimes paired with a 9mm Browning automatic. The younger men in my section were all armed with the NATO 7.62mm SLR rifle. Try as I might, I could not get them to accept the 9mm SMG, which was the perfect weapon for close-quarter combat in a built-up area. The SLR had such power that, if you fired at a man inside a house, the round could go through the front wall, the target, and straight out the back wall again.

Once or twice, I went out on foot patrol with my section to see how they operated. To a man, they thought me foolish for carrying only a 9mm Browning pistol. But I told them: "How can you stop and check people, take names and addresses, and write it all down if you're lugging around a three-foot rifle that takes both hands to hold?"

They didn't answer but I could see their knuckles becoming whiter as they clung onto their SLRs.

Having now been through the duty system twice, it was decided to send me off on a Terrorist Recognition Course to the depot of the Intelligence Corps in Ashford in Kent. It was an intense programme that gave us the basic skills to describe people so that others could recognise them. It was also useful for producing pen portraits of "interesting" individuals to accompany photographs issued to the troops. The course ended with all of the students let loose in Ashford town centre and told to trace and follow a person, based only on their description, without being seen or recognised. All good fun really, but it had a serious purpose.

At the "school" itself, they had displays on the wall of incidents involving troops in Northern Ireland. One disturbing picture showed a human hand lying on the grass verge of a road. It was not until I read the accompanying description that I realised it belonged to one of our lads, murdered by a bomb on the outskirts of Londonderry the previous year. He had been a great mate of mine, and we had attended a Map Reading Instructors Course together at Hermitage near Newbury a few years earlier, enjoying several good nights out.

When I returned from Ashford, I was able to give detailed descriptions of the "players" who passed through the checkpoints at Muff, Moville, or Letterkenny.

One particular day at Letterkenny, a situation arose that needed my attention. The Ulster Defence Regiment (UDR) soldiers guarded all the checkpoints. The checkpoint commander was a UDR SNCO, while we, as RMP NCOs, controlled the flow of traffic in and out. I noticed heightened alertness among the soldiers when a certain car joined the queue. When it was finally called forward, there was an extended conversation between the UDR soldier and the driver. I sensed something was off, so I signalled for the car to be pulled over and directed to the inspection area.

The driver had been asked to open the boot, but he refused. This made the UDR men even more suspicious, especially as the man was a well-known Republican. I was asked to intervene. As I approached, I recognised the driver as someone suspected of being a senior member of the IRA. The situation was explained to me, and I requested that he open the boot. He refused. I then asked for the car keys, which he handed over.

"Do you mind if I open the boot?" I asked. "No, go ahead," he replied.

"Just one thing," I said. "You stand next to me while I do it, so if there is anything in there that will go "bang" it will damage both of us. OK?"

He laughed at that and mumbled something like, "Typical British way out of a situation."

Of course, there was nothing untoward in the boot; the driver was just being awkward. He went on his way and smiled at me as he drove past. There was probably an Armalite under the bonnet!

Who was this man?

James Martin Pacelli McGuinness.

One of the skills we had to learn was facial recognition and, if you like, frequency of appearance – that is, how often you saw somebody. I had noticed when on the Letterkenny checkpoint that on a certain day early in the evening a young woman would come walking towards the checkpoint from the south and, after maybe saying "hello", would walk down the road towards the City Centre. About 2300 hrs at night she would come walking back.

One evening I decided to stop her and have a chat. It had been a quiet day. She stated that her name was Deirdre and she lived just over the border in Carrigans. I asked her what she was going into the city for, as it seemed a regular occurrence. Did she have an evening job? Was she meeting someone? She got rather coy and finally explained that she was in the Territorial Army (TA) as a member of the North Irish Horse Signals Squadron. In fact, she was actually on her way into the very barracks, Clooney Base, that I lived in! As this was, as they say, a fair dander from her home to the base, we arranged that in future, if I were off duty in the base, I would give her a lift back over the river to the checkpoint.

Having done this several times, we became friends and I used to take her into the Mess for a drink before dropping her home. It was all very innocent, just another one of those anomalies in Northern Ireland – that a girl from the Republic was in a Northern Ireland Army unit.

Of course, it had to stop. On all the checkpoints in Northern Ireland was a computer system known as Operation Vengeful, which contained a database of all vehicles registered in Northern Ireland plus many more registered in the Republic. If a registration number were entered into the machine, it would come back with a series of answers that ranged from "nothing; no interest" to "STOP. Arrest all occupants". The CSM who had been checking the printouts from the Op Vengeful system had noticed my car registration number. As "going over the river" to Derry City was out of bounds, I was told to stop doing it with immediate effect. End of short friendship.

Early one morning, as I was coming to the end of a night duty on the Letterkenny checkpoint, I saw a young man walk into the checkpoint from the direction of the Creggan estate above the city. I asked him where he was going, and he said he was a soldier in the Irish Army and on his way to Letterkenny to his barracks. He was catching the Bus Éireann from the checkpoint to Letterkenny. I said to him, "Why not join the British Army? It's a lot closer." He replied, "Join the British Army coming from the Creggan!!" I got his point and wished him a peaceful day at work.

As Easter 1985 approached, Alison informed me that she was going skiing in Austria with some of her colleagues from the Postgraduate Certificate of Education (PGCE) course. I was going to be in Newport, Wales, attending the wedding of my best friend Chas Harrison. Chas had been a rock when I was going through my divorce, and when he was teaching in Hertfordshire, he lived in a big house with three other guys on Aldenham Reservoir near Watford. He was teaching at the Francis Coombe Comprehensive School in North Watford. His fiancée was Lucy, a nurse from Newport whom Chas had met on a ski trip and who was working in St Thomas Hospital in London.

Weekends at Reservoir House became an oasis of fun, parties, visits to pubs and occasional rugby for nearby St Albans (Old Verulamians).

The wedding went off very well, and as Alison was in Austria, I invited the ex-wife of a Royal Military Police friend, Mark Layton, to come with me.

In the meantime, I continued with my duties as a section Sgt, but several incidents marred what would have been a nice ending to my time in Northern Ireland. When my platoon was in that sector of the rota that was based on patrols around the Waterside and Gobnascale areas of Londonderry, I, as the Sergeant, would man the Operations Room assisted by a female Junior Non-Commissioned Officer colleague.

This consisted of day and night duties. One of the things that the Orderly Sergeant, as he was known, had to do was to ensure that the Corporal's Mess was closed at the appropriate time. In practice, this meant that the Corporal's Mess barman would close the bar as such and bring the cashbox to the Duty Room to be placed in the safe. The time that this happened was recorded, and as far as anyone was concerned, the bar was "closed". In practice, the bar stayed open for a long "drinking-up time", as the Corporal's Mess was the only safe place for off-duty men to let their hair down. Londonderry City was out of bounds as it was across the bridge from the base and into the dodgy part of the city. Too many off-duty soldiers had been killed whilst in places they should not have been.

Later that evening, one of the Sergeants found one of our cooks in the corridor of the Sergeant's Mess accommodation. When asked why he was there, he explained that he was making a telephone call to his relatives in England. Asked why he was doing it at such a late hour of the night, he replied that he couldn't make the call on the Corporals" Mess telephone because of all the noise. It didn't take the Regimental Sergeant Major long to work out that the Corporal's Mess was in fact "open" when it should have been "closed". As the

Chapter 18 - We Only Have to Be Lucky Once

Orderly Sergeant for that evening, I was called to account for the situation, and the Regimental Sergeant Major decided to charge me. I pleaded guilty to negligence and was awarded a "three-month warning order", which meant I had to be good for the next three months or face dismissal or demotion.

Following the incident that I have just outlined, the next time I was Orderly Sgt I decided to visit the Corporal's Mess whilst it was still open to remind them to close on time and hand in the cashbox. As laid down in the orders for the Orderly Sgt, I was armed with a 9mm pistol to "defend the operations centre in case of attack". Highly unlikely, but rules are rules. So I walked into the Cpl's Mess in uniform and, as is customary, took my hat off to show I was temporarily "off duty" so that I might have a drink of Coke or similar and chat to the troops.

As I was standing talking to two of the troops, I glanced over one of their shoulders to see an unknown female dressed in civilian clothes (not one of the military girls) open her handbag and pull out a small automatic pistol. I immediately shouted at everyone to lie down on the floor and drew my pistol, which I immediately cocked. I pointed it at the now terrified young girl and told her to put the pistol on the floor. Everyone around me was busy taking cover or lying on the floor. The young girl did not move, just stood there with the pistol in a non-threatening pose. I shouted at her again to put the pistol on the floor.

Just then a young man in civilian clothes, not someone I recognised, stepped into my line of sight and shouted that the pistol was his; he was an off-duty RUC Constable and had asked the young lady to look after his personal protection weapon whilst he was in the Mess. He quickly took the pistol from the girl and put it on the floor. I approached him and asked him for his identity, and he produced his RUC Warrant Card. The young girl was now in tears and it was obvious she had had too much to drink. The RUC Constable apologised profusely and said he would take her, and the pair of them would leave immediately. I allowed him to collect his pistol, girlfriend, and leave.

The moral of the story: don't give your personal protection weapon to someone who should not have it.

My final deployment to the Fermanagh/Monaghan border area was to the town of Aughnacloy. The checkpoint there was right in the middle of the town and manned by soldiers from the Royal Regiment of Fusiliers (RRF) together with the RUC. Royal Military Police once again were acting as information gatherers. The Security Forces (SF) base was about 150 yards from the RUC station, and because our shift patterns did not match, I occasionally found myself walking across to the RUC station on my own. I was not too worried about it as I was armed to the teeth. The RUC would then give me a lift to the checkpoint about a quarter of a mile away in an armoured police car. Once again it was four hours on and eight hours off.

Aughnacloy PVCP (Permanent Vehicle Checkpoint) shows the tower on the left where Aidan McAnespie was shot and killed from

Shortly after I completed my four-week stint and left the place, a well-known "person of interest" as the security forces would call him, and suspected IRA member Aidan McAnespie was accidentally shot dead by a member of the Grenadier Guards who was carrying out his first day of checkpoint duties in the tower.

The soldier claimed that the gun had gone off accidentally. But I would state that there was nothing wrong with the weapon and the soldier was engaged in something we all did from time to time. That was sight someone with our weapon and then pretend to shoot them. The problem was in this instance when he pulled the trigger, he had forgotten that the weapon safety catch had been moved from "Safe" to "Fire."

INCORRECT USE OF WEAPONS

Let me break down some details on the shooting of Aidan McAnespie at Aughnacloy. Whilst it cannot be proved, I hope that, having now seen and understood the different operating procedures connected with the main weapons of the British Army during the Troubles, you may well now form your own opinion on what happened. It was either a case of total mishandling of the GPMG by the Guardsman accused, or he was not supposed to be in charge of that weapon and had gone up into the watchtower to have a look over the land. He then chose to "draw a bead" on Mr McAnespie with the GPMG, which he did not know the state of. As Mr McAnespie walked through the checkpoint, and after drawing a bead on Mr McAnespie, the soldier, incorrectly, squeezed the trigger. He did not check the state of the weapon, which I believe had the belted ammunition already loaded, and the weapon had been made "Ready". The Safety Catch would not have been set to Safe as it should have been. It was not murder, but manslaughter, because the soldier had carried out an incorrect or negligent drill. As it was, the bullet that killed Mr McAnespie was a ricochet off the road behind him which unfortunately hit him in the back.

One of the safest weapons was the 9mm pistol. The requirement to remove the magazine was a good safety feature.

The SMG was the weapon most prone to negligent discharges. The fixed firing pin and the tendency not to pull the working parts fully to the rear before letting them go resulted in several negligent discharges to my knowledge. One handling error personally known to me ended in a tragedy.

A young married man, during the period when it was allowed, had his issued SMG at home. His wife stated that she was nervous about it and, to demonstrate the fact that with the Safety Catch on Safe and even with a loaded magazine attached, the weapon could not be fired, he did the following. He fixed a loaded magazine to the weapon, then made it Ready, then, turning the weapon around to point it at himself, he applied the Safety Catch to S for Safe. You will recall that to do this, the Safety Catch had to be moved completely to the rear. In turning the weapon upon himself and moving the Safety Catch to what he believed was the rear, he was moving the Safety Catch to fully automatic. He then operated the trigger and fired two rounds, which entered his head, killing him instantly. The young soldier is buried in Blaris Cemetery in Lisburn.

The above paragraph deals with the problems encountered with the SMG. However, there were also several incidents involving the Light Machine Gun (LMG) being unloaded in a sangar or defensive location that fired off rounds without the trigger being applied. This was because the excessive machining connected with converting the WW2 'Bren Gun' into the LMG had made the weapon unsafe. The WW2 version of the Bren gun used rimmed .303 cartridges. Anyone who has seen a picture of a Bren gun will note the curved magazine on top of the weapon. This was because the .303 cartridge had a rimmed base making the base of the cartridge bigger than the bullet end. If 30 of the .303 cartridges were stacked one on top of the other, it produced that now familiar curved magazine to hold them.

The LMG being derived from the Bren gun underwent extensive re-machining in order to take the rimless 7.62mm cartridge, which had a narrow base and hence a straighter magazine. The machining was such that the sear, which held the working parts of the gun to the rear when it was cocked, was very thin and unable to hold back the working parts. As the first move was to cock the weapon with the magazine on, this resulted in several Negligent Discharges (ND)s. If a soldier carried out incorrect or dangerous drills when handling loaded weapons, it could result in the unintended discharge of a live round. The soldier would then be placed on a charge for causing a Negligent Discharge. Fines could be imposed depending on the severity of the outcome of a loaded weapon being inadvertently discharged. After at least a dozen such incidents of the LMG apparently being fired and the soldier claiming he had carried out the correct drills, an officer well known to me caused the weapons to be withdrawn and checked by the armourers. Extensive tests proved that the weapon and not the operator was at fault. At least the soldiers involved were reimbursed for the money they had been fined for having an ND. In another incident involving an LMG, as it was being dismounted from its firing position, it was dropped and, on the butt hitting the floor of the sangar, it produced enough force for the working parts to move far enough to strip a round from the magazine and fire it. The soldier was fortunate not to be killed but had two entry and exit wounds in his right arm, one below the elbow and one above. He was also found not to be at fault.

CHAPTER 19

Time for a Change

A couple of months later, the Royal Military Police in Lisburn near Belfast challenged the Royal Military Police in Londonderry to a rugby match. It was played in Londonderry and afterwards there were the usual drinks in the Mess. I was Orderly Sergeant that night, and so I just had the one pint. As I had been voted worst player on the pitch, unknown to me the drink had been spiked. I made my way back to my room, understandably the worse for wear.

Realising what had taken place, and that I was due to go on duty, I had a long cold shower that helped me come around, and managed to get dressed and look the part as I went to take over the night-time Orderly Sergeant duties.

Once all the patrols had been briefed and sent out, I told the young female soldier who was assisting me to answer any phone calls that came in, and just to wake me if they were anything important. This she did until about midnight, when I had to do a routine check of all the weapons held in our unit armoury.

We had been informed that there was a specific threat against our unit and our armoury, which was not the strongest. To counter this, we had placed a Royal Military Police Non-Commissioned Officer within the armoury, armed and with the armoury keys, just in case there was an attack.

I made my way to the armoury and, having identified myself to the Corporal inside, he opened the door and let me in. I proceeded to start my check. This Corporal then asked if it was okay to go and wake his relief whilst I was in the armoury. I agreed and off he went. I was engaged in checking a tray of Walther 7.65 mm automatic pistols used exclusively by the Special Investigation Branch (SIB) and noticed that one section of the tray did not have a weapon in it. On looking at the list I saw that this weapon was assigned to a colleague. I knew from experience that he tended to keep the weapon at home for personal protection. I was therefore less than concerned that it was not there. What I failed to do was to check the sign-out sheet to see if he had signed it out.

I went off duty the next morning and headed into Belfast to have lunch with Alison. Everything was going well until I received a telephone call.

I answered the call and in a commanding voice came, "This is Captain Calder, you need to get your arse back here ASAP." His opening line was followed by, "There is a problem with the weapon count in the armoury."

Very bemused, I got into my car and drove back to Clooney Base. When I arrived at the building housing the armoury and the Sergeant's Mess accommodation, I saw that the place was in uproar. The Officer Commanding took me to one side and said, "The Special Investigation Branch (SIB) Regimental Sergeant Major's pistol is missing. Do you have it?"

I replied that I did not, and then the Officer Commanding informed me that he had to call in the Special Investigation Branch to investigate the possible theft of this weapon. In case you are not aware, I also was now a suspect, and as the evening progressed, my room was searched, and I do mean searched, and I was told not to leave the unit. It is a strange feeling having your colleagues and friends searching your room. I was of course present and informed the search team that if they told me what they were looking for, I could help them find it. They remained tight-lipped and finally went off with the uniform I had been wearing and my boots.

Meanwhile, the accommodation block occupied by the Corporals and other ranks was going to be searched also. At one stage I was approached by two of my Corporals who asked me, "If we hand over spare ammunition that we have, can it be under a no-questions-asked amnesty?"

Knowing that most men kept a few spare rounds of ammunition, because if you lost a round whilst out on patrol it would cost you a £100 fine, I told them it would be okay, whereupon they handed me four SLR 7.62 mm rifle magazines with 30 rounds in each, including tracer rounds.

I handed them in to the Officer Commanding and he then put out a message that there was to be an amnesty and any spare ammunition could be handed in without fear of prosecution. The outcome was that we got about half as much again as the amount of ammunition that had been issued to the unit legally.

I went to speak to the Corporal who had been in the armoury when I went to do my check. I reminded him that I had given him some advice earlier that month when he asked me about replica weapons that he had on the wall in his home in England.

He had been investigated by the Special Investigation Branch on behalf of the Civilian Police in his hometown after they had been told that he had these "weapons". He had not been treated well by the Special Investigation Branch. I told him my career was on the line, and if he had taken the weapon, to just leave it somewhere where it could be found. He assured me he had not taken it.

The next evening, I was sitting in the Sergeant's Mess Dining Room with the Special Investigation Branch Sergeant who was investigating the case, a man named Terry Burroughs, one of the Royal Military Police rugby players on the infamous tour to Hamburg many years before. Just one of those strange coincidences.

Just then the unit Dog Handler entered the room. He explained that he had gone up to the kennels to get his guard dog to start patrolling the camp, and on the door of the kennel he had found a plastic shopping bag. He then produced this, and inside it was the missing 7.65 mm Walther and a spare magazine. There was also a quantity of washing powder, so whoever had left the bag had used it previously to keep their washing items in. Terry immediately told me to stay where I was as he was going to go to my room and seize my box of washing powder. All exceptionally good police work, but I had not taken the weapon. It finally transpired that the Corporal who had been in the armoury on guard had lifted the weapon from the tray and hidden it in his belt under his combat jacket. His reasoning was that he did not like the Special Investigation Branch Regimental Sergeant Major who had questioned him, so he took it to spite him. I was exonerated, but not totally off the hook. I had to appear in front of the Officer Commanding again, and I pleaded guilty once more to negligence, but in mitigation mentioned the spiked drink and the underhanded actions of the Corporal. I was given a second three-month warning order, so the writing was clearly on the wall for me.

The tragic incident of that round of duties was when I was once again Orderly Sergeant. It was a balmy evening, so we had the windows open. At about 2200 hrs we heard the distinct sound of shots being fired close to our base. There were two or three rapid-fire gunshots. On the internal communications system the UDR guard at the front gate then reported that someone had been shot just outside the gate and the perpetrators had made off in a car towards the new Londonderry bridge and over into the Republican side.

Chapter 19 - Time for a Change

I turned the patrol out that was in the base, and they went and secured the scene. That same evening there was an Officer's Mess Cocktail Party in the Mess in Ebrington Barracks, and all the officers from our unit were there. The victim turned out to be a young Private soldier from the Royal Anglian Regiment that was based over the river in Fort George. He thought that he was safe on our side of the river. He had been with a comrade and two girls in a pub on our side of the river a few days before, playing pool. He had his pool cue in a case, and his friend was wearing a distinctive purple leather jacket. When he went to the gents at some time, he thought he was recognised by a known IRA player, and he reported the fact to his chain of command.

He then went back to the same pub a few nights later. However, on this occasion, he asked his friend if he could let him wear the distinctive purple leather jacket. The young soldier, thinking nothing of it, said yes. As they were making their way up the road past Clooney Base, the victim, in his friend's leather jacket, started doing an arms drill with the cue case. This was seen by the gunman who had been waiting in a car.

As the two couples passed the car, the gunman stepped out and fired at the man in the purple leather jacket, killing him instantly. The other three ran in different directions and escaped injury. The RUC turned up at the scene and of course took control of the incident. Information was passed back and forth and somehow the news got to the Officer's Mess Cocktail Party. The Captain and Second in Command with whom I had worked before called me on the telephone to ask what the situation was, and I told him. He stated that everyone in the Mess was told to stay there, so no one could get out to come to the Ops Room. That was okay as the situation was under control. As I put the telephone down it rang again, and it was the Officer Commanding of the Special Investigation Branch sounding the worse for drink. He was at the Cocktail Party.

"Sergeant, I order you to send a car here to collect me so I can go to the scene," he demanded. I politely said "No", mainly because I did not have any patrol vehicles available but also because I did not want the RUC to be confronted by a drunken Special Investigation Branch Royal Military Police officer trying to tell them what to do. During the next half-hour he rang about a dozen times, and each time I turned him down.

Finally, I rang the Second in Command back and asked him to do something about it. He told me not to worry and that he would. I did not get disturbed again that night. The next day I was summoned to the Officer Commanding Special Investigation Branch's office, where he delivered a rebuke to me about not providing him with transport. He did state that he understood I was busy and that there might not have been any vehicles available, but I should have sent one when things had calmed down and a vehicle was available. I apologised for that error, and that was the end of the matter.

What I did not tell him was that the Second in Command had briefed me just before I saw him to tell me that my own Officer Commanding had torn strips off the Special Investigation Branch Officer Commanding for interfering. He told me just to apologise and that would be the end of the matter. Great officer, the Second in Command.

I do love rugby, and I did manage to get some playing time in on my days off. As it was forbidden for troops to cross the River Foyle into Derry City Centre itself, I could not play for City of Derry Rugby Football Club.[38] I was invited to go along the coast a bit and play for Limavady Rugby Football Club. This I did. On one occasion we had an away match in Belfast playing Malone Rugby Football Club. We, that is the local Limavady players and one or two troops from Londonderry, piled into cars and off we went. Naturally, we went via the Glenshane Pass, which was out of bounds to us, but to normal civilians not a problem. We just went with the flow.

---

[38] The club was established in 1881, winning the Irish Provincial Towns Cup in the following season.

Chapter 19 - Time for a Change

We played the match and, on the way back, now about 2000 hrs at night, one bright spark thought it would be a great idea to call into the "Highest Pub in Ireland." He had never been there. Not wanting to make a fuss I stayed quiet. As shared earlier, the area was renowned for Republican sympathisers, so not to advertise my background, I kept my mouth shut.

Inside the pub someone got me a pint and I sat quietly in the corner with the team. Even when one is trying to be discreet there is always that one person that opens their mouth, and open it they did. One of the Limavady players piped up, "Hey, Chippy, you are very quiet. You usually have a joke or a song or two about now!" I looked at him over the top of my glass and said, "Remember who I am and what I do for a living; remember where we are, and put two and two together." He immediately stood up and said loudly, "OK boys, drink up, we are off!" He apologised later, but I told him it was OK, and that I was not going to stand up and start singing in that area.

In April 1985, Alison and I decided to take my next two week's leave outside of Northern Ireland. My brother and his wife, now living in Jersey, offered us the use of their house in St Helier if we would cat-sit their two moggies, Cagney and Lacey. We said we would and off we went. We had a great time there. We did all the tourist bits, visited Elizabeth Castle and the Underground Hospital, and we took the hydrofoil to St Malo and spent the day there soaking up French atmosphere, wine and cheese. I had decided that this would be the best place to buy an engagement ring for Alison, but no matter what jewellery shop we visited, she didn't see anything. Later she would tell me she had set her heart on a small diamond ring she had seen in Belfast.

I had seen lovely rings in Jersey for as much as £35! We had told Alison's mother that my brother and his wife were in Jersey, and we were staying with them. Alison's mother was extremely strict that way. Of course, they were both in Spain, but when they returned, we made sure we took a photo of Alison and them in St Helier town centre to "prove" they were there. Alison and I sat and talked about what the future might hold. I was prepared to quit the Royal Military Police and look for alternative employment in Hertfordshire, in the local constabulary, if she was going to move back to England.

We also discussed our commitment to each other, and on May 10, 1985, we placed the announcement of our engagement in the Daily Telegraph. You can't get more formal than that! So much for me trying to save some money! On May 25, 1985, I parted with £200 for an aquamarine and six-stone diamond ring from Corry's of Belfast.

As I had continued my Open University studies in Northern Ireland, which I had started in Germany, I was required to go to Summer School again. I had kept up with the studies, even going to the extent of writing essays using my bunk bed as a table in the sleeping accommodation of the compound in Fermanagh.

The compound checkpoint was a breeze-block enclosure about 40 yards square. Inside there were three portacabins: one for the infantry section who ran the checkpoint, one for us three Royal Military Police Non-Commissioned Officers, and a further portacabin that housed a kitchen and the ablutions. The side of the enclosure that ran parallel with the road had a combined control tower and cubicle built one metre from the outside wall. There was a gap in the wall to allow one person at a time to walk from the compound out onto the road. The tower was split-level with a General-Purpose Machine Gun (GPMG) mounted in the tower. In the cubicle space below was the radio equipment, the system for monitoring the sensors strung along the border that activated if people walked past them, the 40 mm grenade launcher, and the box of illumination rockets. There were usually two infantrymen squeezed in there as well.

Graham on the wall of the checkpoint on the Rosslea to Monaghan Road. The tower housing the GPMG and surveillance equipment is behind his left shoulder

I rang the Open University to ask once again to go to Bath, but I explained that as I was in the Army, I had to use my annual leave entitlement to attend Summer School. I also asked if it were possible for me to bring my girlfriend, Alison, with me, as this would be the only chance for a sort of holiday that year. Pure cobblers, of course, but the Open University came through and allowed Alison to come with me and even gave us a double room on the university campus. This time I was studying the Technology Foundation course, and it was the opposite of the Arts Foundation course, i.e. more men than women. The good news is that Alison could attend the lectures with me, which did prove to be hilarious at times. Like all students and lecturers, we had to wear a name badge. Mine was just my name but, of course, on Alison's was Dr Alison Farris – Visitor. Many and oft were the times she was approached by fellow students and asked to explain some aspect of the course. Others thought that I had "got off" with one of the Open University lecturers and she was helping me to get an honours degree. As it was, we had fun on campus and tried to see as much of Bath as we could on our days off.

On return from Summer School, I was back at Londonderry City and an incident took place on the road between Londonderry and Strabane. We had received intelligence that a cache of IRA weapons was going to be moved between two locations. Therefore, it was decided to set up a surveillance in a field where it had been worked out that anyone on foot would have to go if they wanted to remain covert. The local infantry battalion sent men out into the field just as it was getting dark, and they dug in and set up sensors and other smart bits of kit to monitor the route that they believed was to be used.

It was a very quiet night and early in the morning, movement was sensed coming towards the dug-in soldiers. It was about 0200 hrs. What turned out to be a group of three people approached the site. The soldiers then identified themselves and called upon the three unknown persons to stop, stand still and raise their hands. Immediately all three adopted various poses whereby the weapons, rifles as it turned out, were brought up to the shoulder in preparation to open fire. In a short burst of gunfire, all three of the unknown persons lay on the ground dead. Was it shoot-to-kill, as the Republican propaganda promoted? No. The soldiers had night vision equipment, and this military night vision was as if one was looking through a camera in daytime.

When it came to identifying who they were, it turned out to be three young men, all aged between 17 and 20. They were each carrying a rifle, three various types of rifles, and it was quickly noticed that each rifle had a piece of coloured sticky tape around the barrel. The same-coloured sticky tape was also wrapped around the magazine on each weapon.

For many of the readers that may not mean too much, but for us it showed these three terrorists had only received very rudimentary training, as the magazines and weapons were colour-coded so that they did not get them mixed up. The soldiers were understandably annoyed and upset at this. The immediate action by one of the young men was to try and pull his balaclava mask down over his face before he started shooting. He never had a chance. Someone in authority had sent these armed terrorists out at night to take on the professional soldiers of the British Army.

There could only have been one outcome.

> **As reported by the Newsletter, Friday, April 5, 1985…**
>
> The three IRA men shot dead by soldiers in Strabane two months ago had been part of a five-man gang who had planned to ambush police.
>
> Details of the event leading up to the shooting were given during an unsuccessful bail application by 21-year-old Declan John Crossan at the High Court in Belfast yesterday.

Crown Counsel claimed that on February 23 last, that Crossan met four other IRA men at Innisfree Gardens in Strabane. They were armed with three rifles, two grenade launchers and grenades, he said.

Counsel alleged the five planned to ambush a police Land Rover by firing grenades at it and if police disembarked from the vehicle, they were to be shot.

However, the police failed to show and Crossan and another man left IRA men Charles Breslin and brothers David and Michael Devine to return their weapons to a hide, it was alleged.

The Hump

In addition to the checkpoints around Londonderry, we had another checkpoint to man in Strabane. This was known as "The Hump Permanent Vehicle Checkpoint" because it was located on slightly rising ground just our side of the border bridge with the Republic. The base was using what had been the old railway station at Strabane, and one could see the remains of a railway bridge going over the Foyle at that point. Strabane was a strong Republican base, and being out on one's own was another aspect of the threat.

On this Permanent Vehicle Checkpoint, roles were reversed, and it was the RUC who controlled who they checked, and they would only call on us if a vehicle search were required. The vehicle was driven into a shed, and we would search it. On occasions, it was a small van carrying copies of the Republican newspaper *An Phoblacht*. I always used to ask if I could have a copy, and then I would make out that I could read it. Again, all part of the game.

Chapter 19 - Time for a Change

On December 22, 1985, I was due to go out to the checkpoint at Letterkenny when a colleague asked me to swap with him at the Hump Permanent Vehicle Checkpoint. The reason was that he wanted to get away early the next morning, and as the Hump crew had to drive back from Strabane, he would be an hour behind everyone else. I had no objection, and so, accompanied by a Corporal, I drove from Londonderry to Strabane in a civilian, unmarked car. When we arrived, we relieved the previous crew and settled down in our room within the Security Force base.

We were then briefed by the UDR Senior Non-Commissioned Officer that they would be evaluating the mortar bomb alarm, because information had become known that there was a distinct possibility of a mortar attack on the Hump.

The day passed off quietly, and that evening after dinner, the Corporal and I were sitting in our room when we heard four loud and distinct "whumps" close by. We immediately grabbed our rifles and dashed out of the door as the mortar attack alarm went off… Can I say at this point, some thirty seconds after the bombs had landed, the alarm went off. The UDR Senior Non-Commissioned Officer just scratched his head when he saw the pair of us huddled behind a concrete wall and shouted, "Get back into your room!"

He was politely and firmly told that we wanted to stay where we were. About ten minutes later, the all clear was sounded, and we began to move about again in relative safety. The four homemade mortar bombs, for that was what the "whump" was, had landed just outside the compound and had failed to explode. The border crossing was shut for the night by the An Garda Síochána on the Republican side and by us on our side. With no traffic to worry about, we then went to bed and slept the sleep of free men.

The Weapons Intelligence team kindly sent me photographs after the attack. The reason for the bombs failing to explode was that the Cordex explosive cable wrapped around the explosive charge had deteriorated with age and failed to initiate. Three plastic bags in the bombs contained the homemade explosive, which fortunately had not detonated.

The mortar baseplate with launch tubes mounted in the back of an open lorry.

The 'Hump' Permanent Vehicle Checkpoint from the Republic side of the bridge. The marked area highlights a white square that was the aiming point for the mortar.

The same view taken in April 2025, showing the Hump Checkpoint as a petrol station.

I spent Christmas 1985 moving between Londonderry and Belfast as I celebrated it with the Company in Londonderry and with Alison in Belfast. She was home from her school, Queenswood in Potters Bar, and we were both preparing to wave "goodbye" to Northern Ireland in January 1986.

She would be going back to Potters Bar, and I would be on my way to a short posting to London. So, for the second time in my life, I prepared to leave Northern Ireland. This time, I thought, except for visiting the in-laws, there would be no other reason to return. A new chapter in life; a new job and… getting married.

"86 was looking like an extremely exciting year as I decided that I would terminate my career with the Royal Military Police, having discussed the matter with Alison. You see, she already had me in training: approval from the wife (future wife) – happy life.

I presented my written application to give notice and the Regimental Sergeant Major immediately called me to his office.

"Do you really want to do this?" he asked.

"Yes, Sir," I replied. "Well, if you withdraw it, I can get you a posting to Hong Kong," he said.

It dawned on me that the Corps was losing senior soldiers at a fast rate, and there was every effort being made to retain people, even old reprobates like me.

"No, thank you, Sir," I said. "I think I can see the writing on the wall. It is time for a change of career."

"Ah well," he said, "it's just as well. You have let yourself down, the Corps, and your father as well."

What a miserable person, I thought: one minute dangling a carrot, the next slagging me off. If I had any doubts in my mind, the Regimental Sergeant Major helped me dismiss them quickly. I left his office knowing I had made the right decision.

But we had one more bridge to cross, Alison and I. It was early in the New Year and Northern Ireland got hit with several days of gale-force storms and high seas. We sat it out in Alison"s house in Belfast, and after four frustrating days, we finally took the ferry from Larne to Stranraer. I was going to have four weeks of civilianisation working in a school with Chas Harrison in Watford, and Alison was going to be in her school in Potters Bar. Eventually, in April 1986, I reported to the HQ of Hertfordshire Constabulary. I received my new blue uniform and was sworn in as a Constable. I began my police training at Ashford on April 7, 1986, having left military life behind me forever. Or so I thought!

Epilogue

Graham and Alison's wedding day, August 23, 1986

Every dangerous tour to Northern Ireland was worth it for the love of my life, Alison Chipperfield – my girl who became my lady, my wife, and my anchor through decades of service.

After completing my military police service, I served as a Police Constable in Hertfordshire from 1986 to 1991, during which I earned my BA(Hons) from the Open University in 1990. Concurrently, I was commissioned as a Lieutenant in the Royal Military Police Territorial Army, attached to the Royal Military Police Provost Company in Catterick – a fortuitous posting, as the Officer Commanding was my former Second in Command from Londonderry, ensuring mutual respect and understanding. In August 1986, as the photograph shows, I married my beloved Alison.

During my constabulary service, I applied to join the Firearms Unit but was rejected because it would be "politically embarrassing" should headlines read "Ex Army Police Constable shoots robber." However, I successfully joined the Explosive Search Team, where my concurrent TA service proved invaluable. The Constabulary's disapproval of TA members meant I was denied unpaid leave for Annual Camp – a restriction that would later influence my career decisions.

At 37, with Alison's unwavering support and blessed with two daughters born in 1987 and 1989, I successfully rejoined the Armed Forces through the Royal Air Force. After graduating as a Pilot Officer from RAF College Cranwell in 1991, I embarked on a distinguished 15-year RAF career, rising to Flight Lieutenant.

Our family flourished during these years of service across multiple continents. We were stationed at RAF Brampton in Huntingdon, Joint Headquarters Rheindahlen in Germany, RAF Benson in Oxfordshire, RAF Manston in Kent, RAF Mount Pleasant in the Falklands, RAF Akrotiri in Cyprus, and finally HQ 4 Mech Brigade in Osnabrück, Germany, in 2007.

Transitioning from military to civilian service, I secured employment as a UK-based Civil Servant, serving as a Staff Officer in Army HQ Osnabrück. Following the military drawdown in 2009, I transferred to HQ 102 Logistic Brigade in Gütersloh, where we spent eight wonderful years in Germany while our daughters pursued their university education in Northern Ireland.

Epilogue

When the Gütersloh garrison closed in 2015, Alison and I returned to Northern Ireland, where I had secured a position within the local garrison. After our professional relationship concluded in late 2016, we embraced civilian life in our home just outside Crumlin, County Antrim.

Today, we are blessed to witness our daughters in loving, secure relationships. I am the proud grandfather of two grandsons – remarkably born on the same day in the same hospital in Antrim – and a granddaughter who delightfully chose to arrive on my birthday.

As I often reflect, my family has always excelled at creating beautiful symmetries in life's tapestry.

SECTION THREE

Weapons Used During Operation Banner

Operation Banner was the code name for the British Armed Forces longest continuous deployment, operating in Northern Ireland from August 14, 1969, to July 31, 2007, during "The Troubles". Its primary objective was to support the Royal Ulster Constabulary (RUC) in maintaining law and order amidst civil unrest and paramilitary violence, a role that evolved over its nearly four-decade duration.

It was the longest continuous deployment in British military history, lasting nearly 38 years and involving over 250,000 military personnel. The number of troops deployed peaked at around 21,000 in the 1970s.

British Army Weapons

9MM BROWNING PISTOL

This was the sidearm used by all British Forces during the period from 1964 until late 2000. It was designed and manufactured by Herstal in Belgium before WWII. The Wehrmacht used many captured pistols. It was replaced by the Glock 9mm.

Description: The 9mm Browning has a magazine that is housed within the pistol grip. It has a capacity of 13 rounds of 9mm pistol ammunition. It is a blowback weapon, referring to once the weapon is fired, the recoil from the round leaving the pistol causes the slide on the top of the weapon to blow back towards the rear. This action initially expels the empty case out of the weapon and on-going forward again under pressure from the return spring, the slide strips a fresh round from the top of the magazine and feeds it into the breech. The weapon can then be fired again by pressing the trigger. It cannot be fired on fully automatic.

Safety Features: A unique feature of the weapon is that it cannot be fired unless a magazine is fitted to it. When the last round has been fired, the top slide is held back automatically so that it is possible to look into the breech to confirm it is empty. The empty magazine is then removed and a fresh one loaded. By operating a release catch on the left side of the weapon, the top slide returns to its normal position at the same time loading a fresh round into the breach.

It is possible to "ready" the weapon, which is to pull back the slide and allow a fresh round to enter the breech and then apply the safety catch. This allows the weapon to be carried in a holster or in the hand, fully loaded and ready to fire without having to "ready" the weapon again.

To unload the weapon, first, the magazine was removed, making it impossible to fire off a round accidentally. The top slide was then pulled to the rear, expelling any cartridge in the breech that had been left there. After checking that the breech was clear, the working parts were allowed to go forward. After the working parts were let go, the magazine was replaced and the trigger squeezed off.

STERLING L1A2 9MM SUB MACHINE GUN

The Sterling 9mm Sub Machine gun, known to all who used it as the SMG, is a modern upgrade of the old WWII Sten Gun. The name is derived from the twin gun makers, Sterling and Enfield. The SMG incorporated a safety system that was a vast improvement on the Sten, as was the 30-round magazine. It was standard issue to all troops who were involved with the operation of armoured vehicles, i.e. tanks, because of its small size. The butt system folds down and swings forward to be secured under the barrel by a barrel catch. It was also the standard weapon of the Royal Military Police (RMP) and was primarily a Close Quarter Battle (CQB) weapon.

Description: The SMG was a pure blowback-operated weapon. A breech block housed in the cylindrical body of the weapon incorporated a fixed firing pin and was operated by the blowback of a fired round and a large spring behind the breech block. To make "Ready," the breech block was pulled to the rear by a right sided cocking handle, and was prevented going forward by a metal sear that was in the pistol grip. Once the cocking handle was released, the block was held back ready to fire.

Safety Features: A safety catch located on the left just above the trigger operates in three positions. Fully to rear S, Safe; one push forward to R was Repetition or single shot, and fully forward to A was Automatic fire. The bolt and firing system could not be operated unless the safety catch was on R or A.

Unlike the 9mm Pistol, this weapon could not chamber a round ready to fire at some later stage. With a fixed firing pin, every time the trigger was pulled, the breech block and the fixed firing pin went forward, stripping a round from the side-mounted magazine, feeding it into the breech and firing it. The breech block was then blown back, hence the name, under the recoil of the round, expelling the empty case. If the safety catch was on R, then another round could not be fired until the rigger was pressed again. If on A, then the breech block would continue to load and fire rounds until either the trigger was released or the magazine was empty.

To unload this weapon safely, the Normal Safety Procedures was to put the safety catch to S, then remove the magazine entirely and physically look inside the weapon to ensure there were no rounds lodged inside or loose rounds that may have come out of the magazine. Once the chamber was declared "clear" the working parts of the breech block were allowed to be released forward under control, i.e. not just allowed to go forward under the pressure of the spring, but controlled by holding onto the cocking handle, squeezing the trigger and slowly allowing the breech block to close. The safety catch was then switched to S, showing the weapon was safe.

Problems with the SMG: When making the weapon Ready and the operator had slippery hands or was not doing the drill correctly, the breech block could be released before it engaged the sear. If the breech block were pulled back but then let go before it engaged the sear, it could travel forward, strip a round from the magazine and fire it. Care had to be taken when making the weapon ready.

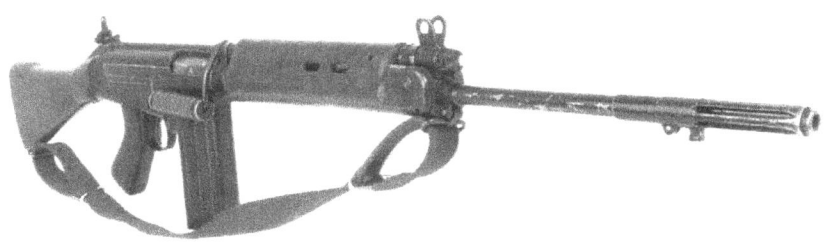

FABRIQUE NATIONAL 7.62MM SELF LOADING RIFLE/ L1A1 7.62MM SLR

This weapon, designed by Fabrique National of Belgium, was taken up by the British Government as the infantry standard weapon after WWII in the late 1950s. It was 7.62mm, equivalent to the old .303" cartridge used during the WWII. Unlike the .303, the cartridge was rimless and therefore took up far less room in a magazine. This will be seen later when the .303" BREN gun was redesigned to take the 7.62mm NATO round and be redesignated Light Machine Gun (LMG). The SLR was replaced in the late 1990s and early 2000s by the 5.56mm SA80 rifle as the infantry standard weapon. Many "old" soldiers saw this as a retrograde step and wanted to retain the SLR, which was a favourite weapon.

Features: The 7.62mm SLR was a gas-operated semi-automatic rifle with a 20-round magazine that could fire both ball and tracer ammunition. Running along the top of the long barrel was a cylinder that housed a gas piston. As the round travelled along the barrel when fired, some of the gases produced by the propellant were diverted upwards by a small hole or port onto the face of the gas piston. This forced the piston backwards, where it engaged with a fully covered breech block and bolt, which housed a movable firing pin. As this breech block and firing pin were forced to the rear, the expended case of the round was ejected out of the chamber to the right. The whole breech block and bolt then moved forward under pressure from a large spring and stripped a round from the magazine and fed it into the breech. It did not automatically fire the new round. This had to be done by the person firing the weapon. First, the trigger had to be released and then activated again to allow an internal hammer to strike the rear of the bolt and impact the movable firing pin against the base of the round. This is why the name Self Loading Rifle is used and not an automatic rifle.

Safety Features: The 7.62mm round fired by the SLR was extremely powerful. In built-up areas, it had been known for rounds fired to go through the front wall of a house and exit out the back. It was not designed for Close Quarters Battle but was supposed to operate at ranges of 300 yards and more. It was also heavy and, being a long weapon, had handling characteristics that made it difficult to mount and dismount from vehicles and it was especially cumbersome in small helicopters like the Gazelle, where it frequently poked out the side windows of the cockpit as it was bundled aboard. Like the 9mm Pistol, this weapon could be made "Ready" and a round lodged in the chamber and left there until it was required to fire it. The cocking handle was on the left side of the weapon and with a 20-round magazine fitted the whole thing was not a light weapon to carry. After making "Ready" the two-position Safety Catch, S or R, was applied to S for Safe. The operator then only had to move the Safety Catch to R and apply pressure to the trigger to fire the weapon. To safely unload the weapon, the Safety Catch was applied, the magazine removed, and the breech block or working parts pulled to the rear once or twice to ensure there were no loose rounds in the chamber. The working parts were then allowed to close on themselves, and the trigger was activated after moving the Safety Catch to R. The magazine was NOT replaced on the weapon under normal circumstances.

7.62MM LIGHT MACHINE GUN/BREN GUN

The Light Machine Gun or LMG as frequently referred to was a conversion of the WWII .303 Bren gun. The name comes from a combination of Brno, the weapons manufacturer in Czechoslovakia and the Enfield weapons factory in North London. The LMG could keep up a good rate of fire but was limited by the magazine capacity. In the original .303 version, the magazine was highly curved to take account of the rimmed .303 ammunition. In the 7.62mm LMG the weapon had been highly modified.

The barrel, for instance, was reconfigured to take the 7.62 mm round. The fluted flash eliminator on the end of the barrel was removed and a more modern flash eliminator like that on the SLR was adopted. The magazine, again using a rimless cartridge, was more upright than the .303 version. The capacity was 30 rounds. The bolt and breech block were also re-worked to take the 7.62mm rimless round. Apart from that, the LMG bore a remarkable resemblance to the Bren from which it came.

Features: The LMG was like the SLR in its internal workings. That is a certain amount of "gas" from the propellant of a round that was diverted to a gas cylinder. However, this time the cylinder and its gas piston are located under the barrel and not on top of it. The firing mechanism is also similar in that when the breech block and bolt move forward, a round is stripped from the magazine and fed into the breech where it is immediately fired. The LMG has a fixed firing pin like the 9mm SMG and like the SMG a round cannot be chambered after the "Ready" is ordered, but every time the breech and bolt go forward, a round is fired. The Safety Catch has its own peculiarities.

The S for Safe is in the middle position of a three-position Safety Catch. To the rear on R, the LMG will fire single shots on Repetition. When pushed all the way forward to A, the rate of fire is increased as the weapon is now on fully automatic.

Safety Features: Conversely to all the other weapons, the LMG unloading sequence is unique in that after applying the Safety Catch, the working parts are then drawn to the rear where they lock into position. All this is done before the magazine is taken off. The magazine is then removed. This allows the operator to then look into the breech and ensure that no rounds are left in the chamber. The working parts are then released to go forward under the power of the internal spring and not eased forward as is the case with the SMG. A protective top cover is then slid over the place where the magazine was and a bottom cover likewise, where the expended empty cases fall out during firing.

The reworking of the internal parts of the LMG led to some problems. The sear, which held the working parts to the rear when unloading, was sometimes prone to letting the working parts go forward without any interference from the operator. There were several incidents of so-called "negligent discharge" that happened when the unloading sequence was being exercised. Likewise dropping the weapon on its butt end with the magazine on could also result in an inadvertent firing of the weapon. Many of them were withdrawn from service and engineering rectification was carried out.

7.62MM GENERAL PURPOSE MACHINE GUN/GPMG

The General-Purpose Machine Gun, or GPMG, was a platoon support weapon. It was usually fired fully automatic in the fire support role. It was also placed in security posts and watchtowers due to its ability to lay down suppressing fire should the location come under attack. It came like the LMG with a fitted bipod but could be mounted on a tripod with the butt removed in a sustained fire role. It used the same 7.62mm round as the SLR and the LMG. It was belt-fed from the left side of the weapon, and the rounds were held together in a self-disintegrating chain link belt. The links of the belt could be collected and used again if there was a need to make up belted ammunition.

Features: The GPMG was a heavy weapon and was usually manned by a 2-man crew, a loader and a gunner. As shown in the picture, it had a carrying handle on the top and a sling for transporting it across the battlefield. However, it was very rarely fired from the carrying position. Like both the SLR and the LMG, the weapon was reloaded using a gas piston positioned under the barrel. However, the internal workings were different as the breech and bolt between them had to strip the round from the linked belt, fire the round, allow the empty case to be ejected and the self-disintegrating chain links to fall clear of the weapon beneath it, before starting the process all over again.

Safety Features: As a belt-fed gun, the GPMG had a different unloading and loading sequence from the other weapons. When the command "Load" was given, a top cover was opened, allowing access to the breech. Several links of the ammunition were then laid into the breech, usually 3 or 4 rounds and then the top cover closed. On "Ready" the weapon was cocked via a handle on the right-hand side of the weapon. The Safety Catch is a push button mounted on the left of the pistol grip. The weapon was usually used in the automatic mode and therefore, bursts of 3 to 5 rounds at a time were the usual method of firing. The "Unload" was like the LMG in that the working parts were pulled to the rear and held back; the top cover was opened and the belted ammunition removed. This allowed the operator to visually check that there were no live rounds or empty cases in the breech before closing the top cover and allowing the working parts to go forward. However, one feature of this weapon did cause some concern. Unlike the 9mm Pistol and the SLR the GPMG could not be charged with a live round in the breech, the weapon then put to Safe and left in such a state with belted ammunition attached. Once the belt was in place, the action of making the weapon "Ready" was for the mechanism to be held to the rear, waiting for the trigger to be pulled. Therefore, if the weapon has a belt of ammunition in place, the working parts can be left locked to the rear and ready to fire. If the weapon then needs to be fired, the Safety Catch is moved to A and then pressure is applied to the trigger.

Terrorist Weapons

The Irish Republican Army (IRA) has a complex and turbulent history, dating back to the early 20th century and the partition of Ireland in the 1920s. Over time, the organisation splintered into various factions, each with differing ideologies and strategies. Among these, the Official IRA (OIRA) emerged as a primarily left-wing group, which gradually scaled back its militant activities during the early years of the Troubles. In contrast, the Provisional IRA (PIRA) became the most prominent and active faction. Widely recognised as the armed wing of Sinn Féin, the Provisional IRA took up arms against the British Government and what it termed the "Crown Forces" – a term used to describe the RUC, British Army, and other government entities, including members of the judiciary and political establishment, past and present.

Many of the weapons that were available to PIRA were, at the beginning of the conflict, those kept "under the bed" from previous campaigns like those carried out during the 1950s or even earlier. It was not until later in the campaign that the PIRA started to re-arm with weapons purchased with funds from sympathisers and misguided Americans who gave freely to NORAID, supposing they were helping the poor and dispossessed in Ireland. Such funds enabled people like Col. Gaddafi of Libya to supply both arms and explosives to the PIRA, along with arms dealers based in the USA. Hence, the proliferation of the AR-15, the Armalite. Only vigilant watch and good intelligence allowed most of these shipments to be intercepted and not allowed to fall into the terrorists' hands.

The following images feature some of the weapons, including "factory-built" alongside others that were crudely assembled in backstreet workshops or small industrial units. It's important to remember that during World War II, the STEN submachine gun – a British military weapon – was largely constructed from simple stamped metal parts. Its basic design demonstrated how easy it could be to mass-produce firearms with limited resources. This reality made the production of homemade weapons entirely feasible, especially during the early years of the Troubles, during which Loyalist paramilitaries were dominant.

9mm Browning Hi-Power Pistol

Belgian Excellence in Northern Ireland's Professional Operations

The Browning Hi-Power pistol – the legendary 9mm semi-automatic designed by John Moses Browning and manufactured by Fabrique Nationale in Belgium – became one of the most prevalent and respected sidearms throughout the Troubles, serving with distinction across all factions involved in Northern Ireland's conflict. This iconic pistol brought exceptional reliability, impressive magazine capacity, and proven military pedigree to the urban warfare environment of Belfast and beyond.

The Hi-Power's tactical superiority made it highly sought after by all parties to the conflict. Its 13-round magazine capacity provided significant firepower advantages over revolvers and smaller pistols, while its 9mm Parabellum chambering delivered excellent stopping power with manageable recoil. The pistol's single-action trigger system offered exceptional accuracy for precision shooting, while its robust construction and simple maintenance requirements ensured reliability under demanding operational conditions.

Republican organisations, particularly the Provisional IRA, acquired Hi-Powers through multiple channels, including European arms networks, theft from security forces, and purchases from civilian sources. The weapon's widespread military adoption and proven combat record made it a preferred sidearm for Republican operatives conducting both urban operations and rural ambushes. Its relatively compact size allowed for effective concealment while maintaining serious combat capability.

Loyalist paramilitaries extensively utilised Hi-Powers, often obtaining them through similar channels, including military surplus, private collections, and criminal networks. The Ulster Volunteer Force and Ulster Defence Association valued the pistol's reliability and firepower for both defensive operations and offensive activities within their communities. The weapon's association with legitimate military forces enhanced its appeal to groups seeking to project professional military capability.

British security forces, including the Royal Ulster Constabulary and various military units, officially adopted the Hi-Power as a standard sidearm, making it ironically common on both sides of the conflict. This dual usage created complex situations where the same weapon model appeared in the hands of both security forces and the paramilitaries opposing them.

The psychological impact of the Hi-Power extended beyond its tactical utility – its military pedigree and association with professional armed forces worldwide made it a symbol of serious military capability rather than amateur insurgency.

.45 ACP Pistol (American Colt Pistol)

American Power in Northern Ireland's Urban Combat

The .45 ACP pistol – encompassing various models including the iconic Colt M1911, Smith & Wesson revolvers, and other American designs – became a cornerstone sidearm throughout the Troubles, bringing devastating stopping power and reliable American engineering to Northern Ireland's conflict. These robust handguns, chambered in the powerful .45 Automatic Colt Pistol cartridge, represented both formidable close-quarters capability and strong symbolic connections to Irish-American support networks.

The .45 ACP's tactical superiority was immediately apparent to paramilitaries familiar with its ballistic performance. The cartridge's large, heavy bullet delivered exceptional stopping power at close range, often incapacitating targets with single hits where smaller calibres might require multiple shots. This lethality advantage proved crucial in the quick, decisive engagements characteristic of urban guerrilla warfare, where operatives needed immediate neutralisation of threats with minimal ammunition expenditure.

Republican organisations, particularly the Provisional IRA, acquired .45 ACP pistols primarily through Irish-American networks and sympathetic veterans who provided both weapons and training. The M1911's association with American military service resonated strongly with Republican operatives, while its proven combat record and rugged construction made it ideal for the demanding conditions of clandestine warfare. These weapons often arrived alongside Thompson submachine guns and other American firearms, demonstrating coordinated procurement efforts.

Loyalist paramilitaries also utilised .45 ACP pistols, often obtaining them through different channels, including military surplus, private collections, and theft from legitimate sources. The Ulster Volunteer Force and Ulster Defence Association valued the cartridge's stopping power for close-quarters operations and intimidation activities within their communities.

British security forces carried various .45 ACP weapons, particularly Special Forces units and military police who appreciated the cartridge's proven battlefield effectiveness. The weapon's substantial recoil and size made it less suitable for general issue but ideal for specialised roles requiring maximum stopping power.

The psychological impact of .45 ACP weapons extended beyond their tactical utility – their association with American military tradition and their devastating close-range effectiveness made them powerful symbols of armed resistance and professional military capability.

7.65mm CZ 70 Pistol

Czechoslovakian Engineering in Northern Ireland's Covert War

The CZ 70 pistol – a compact, blowback-operated sidearm manufactured by Česká zbrojovka in Czechoslovakia – became a notable presence during the Troubles as paramilitaries gained access to Eastern European weapons through evolving international arms networks. This well-engineered pistol brought Warsaw Pact reliability and sophisticated European manufacturing to Northern Ireland's conflict, reflecting the increasingly global nature of weapons procurement as the Troubles intensified.

The CZ 70's tactical advantages lay in its exceptional reliability and compact design optimised for concealed carry. Chambered in 7.65mm Browning (.32 ACP), the pistol delivered adequate stopping power while maintaining minimal dimensions for deep concealment operations. Its simple blowback mechanism and robust construction ensured consistent performance under adverse conditions, while its double-action trigger system allowed safe carry with a chambered round – crucial advantages for covert operatives.

Republican organisations, particularly intelligence units within the Provisional IRA, acquired CZ 70s through Eastern European arms networks that expanded significantly during the 1970s and 1980s. These weapons often arrived alongside other Warsaw Pact firearms, reflecting Republican connections to socialist governments and liberation movements worldwide. The pistol's compact size made it ideal for close-protection duties, assassination operations, and situations requiring absolute concealment within urban environments.

Loyalist paramilitaries encountered CZ 70s less frequently, primarily due to their limited connections to Eastern European arms networks compared to Republican organisations with broader international solidarity movements. When these pistols did appear in Loyalist hands, they typically indicated sophisticated procurement operations or connections to criminal networks with access to Eastern European military surplus.

The weapon's Czechoslovakian origin carried particular symbolic weight during the Cold War period, representing Republican connections to socialist bloc countries opposed to Western imperialism. British security forces regarded CZ 70 seizures as evidence of expanding Republican arms procurement capabilities beyond traditional Western sources, raising concerns about Warsaw Pact support for Irish Republican activities.

The pistol's civilian appearance and European styling made it less conspicuous than military-issue weapons in undercover scenarios, while its reputation for mechanical reliability ensured consistent performance during critical operations where weapon failure could prove fatal.

9mm Parabellum MAB PA-15 Pistol

French Military Engineering in Northern Ireland's Shadow War

The MAB PA-15 pistol – a robust 9mm semi-automatic manufactured by Manufacture d'Armes de Bayonne in France – emerged as a significant sidearm during the Troubles, bringing French military-grade reliability and exceptional magazine capacity to Northern Ireland's conflict. This steel-framed pistol represented sophisticated European procurement networks and demonstrated the international scope of arms trafficking that sustained the decades-long violence.

The PA-15's primary tactical advantage lay in its exceptional 15-round magazine capacity, unusually high for pistols of its era and providing significant firepower advantages over standard 6-8 round sidearms. Its 9mm Parabellum chambering delivered substantial stopping power while maintaining ammunition compatibility with submachine guns and other weapons already in circulation. The pistol's robust all-steel construction and French military pedigree ensured reliability under demanding operational conditions.

Republican organisations, particularly units within the Provisional IRA requiring high-capacity sidearms, acquired PA-15s through continental European arms networks that often-included sympathetic dealers and criminal organisations. These weapons typically arrived alongside other French and European firearms, reflecting the sophisticated procurement operations that Republican groups developed throughout the 1970s and 1980s. The pistol's military origins and professional appearance enhanced Republican credibility as a serious armed organisation.

Loyalist paramilitaries encountered PA-15s less frequently, primarily due to their limited access to continental European arms networks compared to Republican organisations. When these pistols did appear in Loyalist hands, they usually indicated significant arms deals or connections to international criminal networks beyond typical local acquisition methods.

British security forces regarded PA-15 seizures as indicators of sophisticated arms trafficking operations extending deep into European defence manufacturing regions. The weapon's military specification and restricted civilian availability suggested access to professional channels typically reserved for legitimate government customers, raising intelligence concerns about security breaches within European arms industries.

The pistol's distinctive appearance and high capacity made it immediately recognisable to security forces familiar with contemporary military hardware, often triggering intensive investigations to trace supply networks and prevent further acquisitions.

The PA-15's weight and size, while substantial for a pistol, were offset by its superior firepower and reliability advantages in sustained engagements.

7.65mm Walther PPK Pistol

German Precision in Northern Ireland's Covert Operations

The Walther PPK pistol – the compact German sidearm made famous by James Bond films – maintained a distinctive presence during the Troubles as a sophisticated concealment weapon favoured by both security forces and paramilitary operatives. This precision-engineered pistol brought European craftsmanship and reliable performance to Northern Ireland's conflict, serving in roles ranging from personal protection to close-quarters assassination operations.

The PPK's tactical advantages lie in its exceptional compactness and reliability. Chambered in 7.65mm Browning (.32 ACP), the pistol delivered adequate stopping power while maintaining minimal size and weight for deep concealment. Its double-action trigger system allowed for safe carry with a chambered round, while its all-steel construction ensured consistent performance under demanding conditions. The weapon's refined manufacturing and tight tolerances provided accuracy superior to many larger pistols.

Republican organisations, particularly intelligence units within the Provisional IRA, acquired PPKs through European arms networks and specialised procurement operations. The pistol's compact dimensions made it ideal for covert operations, close-protection duties, and situations requiring absolute concealment. Its association with professional intelligence services enhanced its appeal to Republican operatives seeking sophisticated equipment that projected competence and professionalism.

Loyalist paramilitaries also utilised PPKs, often obtaining them through private collections, military surplus channels, or theft from legitimate sources. The weapon's reputation for reliability and its manageable recoil made it attractive to operatives requiring dependable sidearms for protection duties or intimidation operations within their communities.

British security forces, including Special Branch officers and military intelligence personnel, sometimes carried PPKs as backup weapons or for covert operations where larger sidearms would compromise concealment. The pistol's civilian appearance and European origin made it less conspicuous than military-issue weapons in undercover scenarios.

The weapon's cultural cache, enhanced by its cinematic associations, added psychological dimensions to its practical utility. Its appearance in paramilitary hands often indicated sophisticated procurement capabilities and professional operational planning rather than opportunistic weapon acquisition.

The PPK's relatively low-powered cartridge limited its tactical effectiveness compared to larger calibre pistols, but its superior concealability often outweighed firepower considerations in covert operations.

.38 Special

The Workhorse of Both Sides in Northern Ireland's Conflict

The .38 Special revolver was one of the most prevalent handguns throughout the Troubles, appearing in the hands of both security forces and paramilitary organisations. Its widespread availability, reliability, and ease of use made it a cornerstone weapon in Northern Ireland's protracted conflict.

British security forces, including the Royal Ulster Constabulary (RUC) and various military units, commonly carried .38 Special revolvers as standard sidearms. The Webley .38 Mk IV and Smith & Wesson Model 10 were particularly favoured for their proven track record and stopping power. These revolvers offered the reliability that bolt-action mechanisms couldn't match in the unpredictable urban warfare environment of Belfast and Londonderry.

Paramilitary groups on both sides – Republican organisations like the Provisional IRA and Loyalist groups such as the UVF – also heavily utilised .38 Special revolvers. The weapon's simplicity made it ideal for operatives with limited firearms training, while its compact size allowed for easy concealment during operations. Unlike semi-automatic pistols, revolvers rarely jammed and required minimal maintenance, crucial factors for clandestine organisations operating under constant pressure.

The .38 Special's moderate recoil and manageable report made it suitable for close-quarters engagements typical of the urban conflict. Its six-round cylinder capacity, while limited compared to semi-automatic alternatives, was often sufficient for the quick, decisive actions characteristic of paramilitary operations during the Troubles.

Black market acquisition of .38 revolvers was facilitated through various channels, including theft from security forces, importation through smuggling networks, and purchases from criminal contacts in Britain and the Republic of Ireland. The weapon's ubiquity in civilian and law enforcement contexts made it relatively easy to obtain compared to military-grade firearms.

.455 Webley Revolver

A Legacy Weapon in Northern Ireland's Modern Conflict

The .455 Webley revolver, while officially obsolete by the time of the Troubles, maintained a notable presence throughout Northern Ireland's conflict as both a historical artefact and a functional weapon. Originally the British Army's standard sidearm from the 1890s through World War II, these robust revolvers found their way into the hands of various combatants during the decades-long unrest.

The weapon's primary appeal lay in its exceptional stopping power – the .455 Webley cartridge delivered significantly more kinetic energy than the later .38 Special, making it devastatingly effective at close range. This potency, combined with the revolver's legendary reliability and simple operation, made it attractive to paramilitary groups despite its age and weight disadvantages.

Republican organisations, particularly the Provisional IRA, occasionally acquired .455 Webley's through raids on private collections, theft from museums, or purchases from collectors and military surplus dealers. The weapon's historical significance to British military heritage added psychological impact to its tactical utility – using the former sidearm of the British Empire against contemporary British forces carried symbolic weight.

Loyalist paramilitaries also utilised .455 Webley's, often sourcing them from family collections passed down by veterans of the World Wars. Former servicemen's personal weapons, legally held but sometimes diverted to paramilitary use, represented a significant source of these revolvers during the conflict.

The .455's substantial recoil and slower reload time compared to modern firearms limited its tactical effectiveness, but its intimidation factor and devastating close-range impact ensured its continued relevance. Security forces occasionally encountered these weapons during raids, serving as reminders of the conflict's deep historical roots and the diverse arsenal available to irregular combatants.

9mm Glock 17 Pistol

Austrian Innovation in Northern Ireland's Modern Conflict

The Glock 17 pistol – the revolutionary polymer-framed, striker-fired sidearm designed by Gaston Glock in Austria – emerged during the later phases of the Troubles as a cutting-edge weapon representing the evolution toward modern firearms technology in Northern Ireland's conflict. This groundbreaking pistol brought unprecedented reliability, high capacity, and innovative construction to the urban warfare environment, demonstrating the continuous advancement of paramilitary armament throughout the decades-long violence.

The Glock 17's tactical advantages were immediately apparent to operatives familiar with contemporary firearms technology. Its 17-round magazine capacity provided exceptional firepower for a service pistol, while its 9mm Parabellum chambering delivered proven stopping power with manageable recoil. The revolutionary polymer frame reduced weight significantly compared to traditional steel-framed pistols, while the striker-fired action eliminated external hammers and manual safeties, creating a streamlined weapon optimised for rapid deployment.

Republican organisations, particularly modernising units within the Provisional IRA seeking state-of-the-art equipment, acquired Glock 17s through sophisticated European arms networks operating during the 1980s and early 1990s, with a number of them being smuggled from the US following the IRA's 1994 ceasefire.

These weapons typically indicated access to contemporary military and law enforcement suppliers, representing the highest levels of procurement sophistication available to paramilitary organisations. The pistol's adoption by numerous police and military forces worldwide enhanced its appeal to Republican operatives.

The weapon's revolutionary design and modern appearance projected an image of technological sophistication that enhanced Republican credibility as a professional military organisation rather than an amateur insurgent group. Its polymer construction and unconventional appearance sometimes created identification challenges for security forces accustomed to traditional steel-framed weapons.

British security forces recognised Glock 17 encounters as evidence of highly advanced procurement capabilities and access to contemporary defence industry sources. The weapon's recent introduction and limited civilian availability suggested connections to military or law enforcement supply chains, raising significant intelligence concerns about security breaches within European arms industries.

Loyalist paramilitaries rarely encountered these weapons during the period, primarily due to their limited access to cutting-edge European arms networks and the pistol's relatively high cost compared to older, surplus weapons more readily available through traditional channels.

.303 Lee-Enfield Rifle

British Heritage

The .303 Lee-Enfield rifle – the legendary bolt-action weapon that served as the backbone of British forces through two World Wars – became a deeply symbolic and tactically significant firearm during the Troubles, representing both Ireland's complex military heritage and the ironic deployment of British imperial weaponry against contemporary British forces in Northern Ireland.

The Lee-Enfield's enduring tactical value lay in its exceptional accuracy, robust construction, and powerful .303 British cartridge that delivered devastating long-range performance. Its ten-round magazine capacity, unusually high for a bolt-action rifle, provided sustained fire capability superior to most contemporary hunting rifles, while its proven reliability under adverse conditions made it ideal for extended storage in weapons caches and immediate deployment when required.

Republican organisations, particularly the Provisional IRA, acquired Lee-Enfields through multiple channels, including theft from territorial army units, purchases from private collectors, and acquisition from Irish veterans of British military service. The weapon's widespread civilian ownership for hunting and sport shooting made it relatively accessible compared to military weapons, subject to stricter controls. Its .303 ammunition remained commercially available, simplifying logistical requirements for sustained operations.

The psychological impact of Lee-Enfields in Republican hands carried profound symbolic weight – using the former standard rifle of the British Empire against contemporary British forces represented a powerful reversal of colonial power relationships. This symbolism was not lost on either Republican propagandists or British security forces, who recognised the weapon's historical significance to both sides of the conflict.

Loyalist paramilitaries also utilised Lee-Enfields, often inherited from family members who had served in British forces during the World Wars. For Loyalist groups, the rifle represented continuity with their tradition of military service to the Crown, even as they deployed it in illegal paramilitary activities defending their communities.

British security forces encountered Lee-Enfields regularly during weapons seizures, recognising their potential for accurate long-range shooting and their symbolic importance to Republican operations. The rifle's distinctive appearance and ballistic signature made it immediately identifiable to forensic specialists investigating shooting incidents.

The weapon's robust construction and simple maintenance requirements ensured that rifles manufactured decades earlier remained fully functional throughout the Troubles period.

For further interesting information

[i] See endnote.

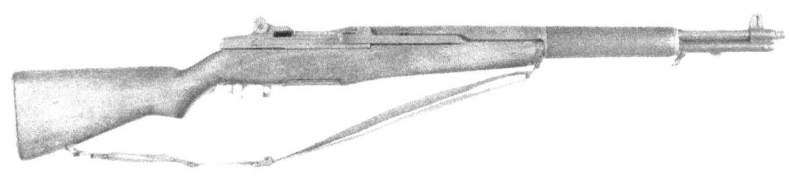

.30-06 M1 Garand Rifle

American Wartime Heritage in Northern Ireland's Conflict

The M1 Garand rifle – the iconic "greatest battle implement ever devised" according to General Patton – maintained a distinctive presence during the Troubles, bringing World War II-era American firepower to Northern Ireland's modern conflict. This legendary semi-automatic rifle, with its distinctive "ping" of the ejecting en-bloc clip, represented both formidable long-range capability and deep historical connections between Irish-America and the Republican cause.

The Garand's tactical advantages were immediately apparent in the Northern Irish context. Its .30-06 Springfield cartridge delivered devastating long-range accuracy and stopping power, making it exceptionally effective for sniper operations and ambushes against security forces. The rifle's eight-round en-bloc clip system, while limiting sustained fire compared to detachable magazines, provided reliable semi-automatic capability with the powerful cartridge that outclassed most contemporary weapons in paramilitary hands.

Republican organisations, particularly the Provisional IRA, acquired Garands primarily through Irish-American veteran networks and military surplus channels. Many weapons were obtained from World War II and Korean War veterans sympathetic to the Republican cause, who either donated their service rifles or facilitated purchases through collector networks. The weapon's legal civilian ownership in the United States made acquisition relatively straightforward compared to military weapons, subject to stricter controls. They were imported to Ireland in large numbers from 1970 onwards and were still in widespread general use in the early 1980s.

The psychological impact of the Garand extended beyond its tactical utility. Its association with American victory in World War II and the liberation of occupied Europe resonated with Republican narratives of national liberation, while its precision and range capabilities enhanced the IRA's reputation for military professionalism. The weapon's appearance in Republican hands symbolised continuity with earlier generations of Irish-American support for armed resistance against British rule.

British security forces treated Garand encounters seriously, recognising the rifle's exceptional long-range accuracy and penetration capability. Its presence often indicated planned sniper operations or ambushes, requiring enhanced countermeasures and tactical responses. The weapon's distinctive report and ballistic signature made it identifiable to forensic specialists investigating shooting incidents.

The rifle's robust construction and simple maintenance requirements made it ideal for extended storage in weapons caches, with many examples remaining functional after years of concealment in harsh conditions.

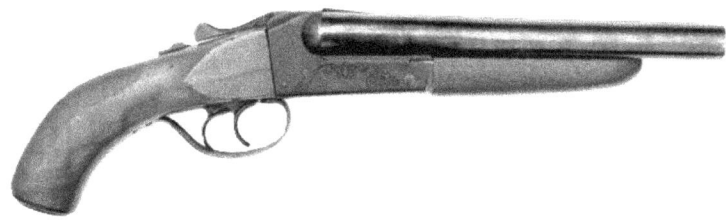

Sawn-Off Shotgun

Loyalist Workshop Modifications for Close-Quarters Terror

The sawn-off shotgun – typically created by cutting down the barrel and often the stock of conventional hunting shotguns – became a signature weapon of Loyalist paramilitaries during the Troubles, representing both practical tactical adaptation and intimidating psychological warfare. These modified firearms, produced in clandestine workshops throughout Protestant areas of Belfast and other Loyalist strongholds, demonstrated the resourcefulness of paramilitaries in adapting civilian weapons for urban combat.

Loyalist organisations, particularly the Ulster Volunteer Force (UVF) and Ulster Defence Association (UDA), systematically modified legally-obtained shotguns by sawing their barrels down to 12-18 inches, dramatically increasing their concealability while maintaining devastating close-range effectiveness. This modification transformed unwieldy hunting weapons into compact, easily hidden firearms perfect for assassinations, intimidation, and close-quarters engagements in Northern Ireland's urban environment.

The tactical advantages of sawn-off shotguns were immediately apparent to Loyalist paramilitaries. Their widespread pattern made precise aiming unnecessary at close range, while their devastating stopping power ensured lethality even with marginal hits. The weapon's compact size allowed operatives to conceal them under coats or in bags, then deploy them rapidly for quick strikes before melting back into civilian populations.

Workshop modifications typically involved more than simple barrel cutting – skilled Loyalist craftsmen often shortened stocks, modified triggers, and sometimes added crude suppressors or other tactical enhancements. These modifications were performed in the same clandestine facilities that produced homemade submachine guns, utilising expertise from Belfast's industrial workforce and ex-military personnel within Loyalist communities.

The psychological impact of sawn-off shotguns extended far beyond their tactical utility. Their association with American gangster culture and violent crime made them powerful intimidation tools, while their crude, improvised appearance conveyed a sense of desperate brutality that terrorised potential targets. The weapons became synonymous with Loyalist death squads and sectarian assassinations throughout the conflict.

British security forces regularly discovered both completed sawed-off shotguns and evidence of modification workshops during raids on Loyalist areas. The weapons' prevalence demonstrated the sophisticated weapons manufacturing capabilities that Loyalist paramilitaries developed when conventional arms proved difficult to obtain through legitimate channels.

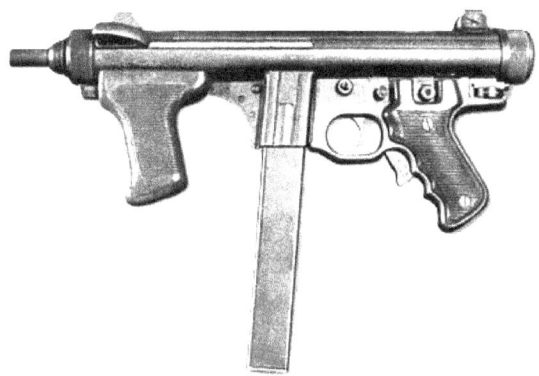

9mm Beretta Model 12 Submachine Gun

Italian Engineering in Ireland's Urban Warfare

The Beretta Model 12 submachine gun, manufactured by Beretta in Italy, represented one of the more sophisticated automatic weapons that occasionally surfaced during the Troubles. This compact, selective-fire weapon brought European military-grade firepower to Northern Ireland's conflict through various smuggling channels and arms deals.

The Model 12's appeal to paramilitary organisations lies in its exceptional compactness and controllability. Its folding stock and short barrel made it highly concealable while maintaining effective automatic fire capability – crucial advantages for urban operations in Belfast's narrow streets and cramped housing estates. The weapon's relatively lightweight construction and manageable recoil allowed operatives to maintain accuracy during sustained bursts, a significant tactical advantage over heavier submachine guns.

Republican groups, particularly the Provisional IRA, acquired Model 12s through continental European arms networks, often alongside other Italian and French weapons. The submachine gun's presence reflected the sophisticated international procurement operations that Republican organisations developed throughout the 1970s and 1980s, utilising contacts in countries sympathetic to their cause or simply willing to profit from arms sales.

The weapon's 9mm Parabellum ammunition was readily available and shared compatibility with various pistols already in circulation, simplifying logistics for paramilitary units. It's 20, 30, or 40-round magazine options provide flexibility between concealment and sustained firepower, making it adaptable to different operational requirements.

British security forces occasionally encountered Model 12s during weapons seizures and post-incident investigations. The submachine gun's appearance in Northern Ireland demonstrated the global nature of the conflict's supply chains and the increasingly militarised character of paramilitary operations as the Troubles progressed.

7.62mm Vz. 58 Assault Rifle

Czechoslovakian Innovation in Northern Ireland's International Arsenal

The Vz. 58 assault rifles – a distinctive Czechoslovakian design manufactured by Česká zbrojovka that superficially resembled the AK-47 but employed fundamentally different engineering – emerged as a significant automatic weapon during the later stages of the Troubles, bringing Warsaw Pact military technology and reliable firepower to Northern Ireland's conflict through expanding Eastern European arms networks.

The Vz. 58's tactical advantages lay in its lightweight construction, exceptional reliability, and powerful 7.62x39mm cartridge shared with the AK-47. Unlike the Kalashnikov's gas-operated system, the Vz. 58 employed a short-stroke piston mechanism that reduced weight while maintaining the stopping power and penetration capability that made Eastern Bloc rifles so effective. Its milled receiver and precision manufacturing provided superior accuracy compared to many stamped-steel contemporaries, making it effective for both automatic fire and precision shooting.

Republican organisations, particularly units within the Provisional IRA seeking to diversify their arsenal beyond traditional sources, acquired Vz. 58s through sophisticated Eastern European arms networks that developed during the 1970s and 1980s. These weapons often arrived alongside other Warsaw Pact firearms, reflecting Republican connections to socialist governments and liberation movements worldwide. The rifle's AK-47 ammunition compatibility simplified logistics while offering a technically superior platform.

The weapon's Czechoslovakian origin carried particular significance during the Cold War period, representing Republican access to advanced socialist military technology and demonstrating the international scope of support for their cause. British security forces regarded Vz. 58 seizures as evidence of expanding Republican procurement capabilities beyond Western sources, raising concerns about Warsaw Pact involvement in Irish Republican activities.

In December 1987, the UVF received a large shipment of weapons, including Vz. 58 assault rifles, Browning Hi-Power pistols, RPG-7 rocket launchers, and grenades.

The rifle's distinctive appearance, while similar to the AK-47, was recognisable to security forces familiar with Warsaw Pact weaponry, often triggering intelligence investigations to trace Eastern European supply networks and assess the extent of socialist bloc support for Republican operations.

.45 ACP/.380 ACP Ingram M10/M11 Submachine Gun

American Firepower in Northern Ireland's Shadow War

The Ingram M10 and M11 submachine guns – compact, high-rate-of-fire weapons manufactured by Military Armament Corporation (MAC) in the United States – occasionally appeared in Northern Ireland during the height of the Troubles, representing some of the most devastating close-quarters weapons available to paramilitary forces.

The M10, chambered in .45 ACP, and the smaller M11, typically in .380 ACP, were prized for their exceptional compactness and overwhelming firepower. With cyclic rates exceeding 1,000 rounds per minute, these weapons could deliver devastating volleys in seconds, making them particularly effective for ambushes, assassinations, and rapid strike operations characteristic of paramilitary tactics.

Republican organisations, especially the Provisional IRA, acquired Ingram's through American fundraising networks and arms smuggling operations. The weapon's association with American organised crime and their availability on the black market made them accessible through Irish-American connections, particularly during the 1970s and early 1980s, when MAC weapons were more readily available before tighter U.S. firearms regulations.

The Ingram's primary tactical advantage was its ability to be easily concealed while delivering submachine gun firepower. Its short barrel and collapsible stock allowed operatives to hide the weapon under coats or in bags, then deploy it rapidly for close-range engagements. However, the weapon's extreme rate of fire also presented challenges – ammunition consumption was rapid, and maintaining control during automatic fire required considerable skill.

Loyalist paramilitaries also occasionally obtained Ingram rifles, though less frequently than Republican groups. The weapon's appearance in Northern Ireland reflected the international arms trade's reach and the sophisticated procurement networks that developed around the conflict, extending from Belfast to New York and beyond.

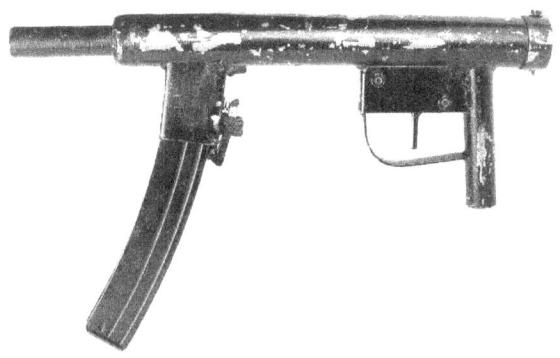

9mm Homemade Submachine Guns

Loyalist Workshop Engineering in Northern Ireland's Conflict

Homemade 9mm submachine guns represented one of the most distinctive and resourceful aspects of Loyalist paramilitary armament during the Troubles. These crude but effective weapons, manufactured in clandestine workshops across Protestant areas of Belfast and other Loyalist strongholds, demonstrated both the ingenuity and desperation of paramilitaries facing arms embargoes and limited international supply networks.

Loyalist organisations, particularly the Ulster Volunteer Force (UVF) and Ulster Defence Association (UDA), developed sophisticated improvised weapons manufacturing capabilities when conventional arms procurement proved difficult. Unlike Republican groups with extensive international connections, Loyalist paramilitaries often relied on local engineering expertise, utilising skilled tradesmen from Belfast's shipyards and engineering works to produce functional automatic weapons.

These homemade submachine guns typically featured simple blowback mechanisms, fabricated from readily available materials including steel tubing, basic machining components, and improvised firing mechanisms. While crude in appearance, many achieved remarkable reliability and effectiveness. The weapons were usually chambered in 9mm Parabellum due to ammunition availability and the cartridge's suitability for simple blowback operation.

Production centres operated in garage workshops and back-room facilities throughout Loyalist areas, with skilled machinists and welders contributing their expertise to the cause. The weapons often incorporated innovative solutions to manufacturing challenges, including improvised suppressors and folding stocks crafted from salvaged materials.

British security forces regularly discovered these workshops during raids, uncovering various stages of production from raw materials to completed weapons. The homemade submachine gun's presence demonstrated the conflict's evolution into a sophisticated guerrilla war, where industrial skills were weaponised and traditional supply chains were replaced by local innovation and determination.

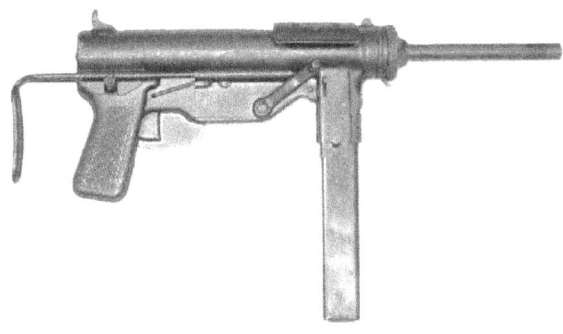

.45 ACP M3 "Grease Gun" Submachine Gun

American Wartime Legacy in Northern Ireland's Streets

The M3 submachine gun, colloquially known as the "Grease Gun" for its crude appearance and resemblance to automotive tools, emerged as a significant weapon during the Troubles despite being a World War II-era American design. This simple, reliable automatic weapon found its way into Northern Ireland through various channels, becoming a formidable presence in the hands of both Republican and Loyalist paramilitaries.

The M3's appeal lay in its exceptional simplicity and robust construction. Originally designed as a cheap, mass-producible alternative to the Thompson submachine gun, its straightforward blowback mechanism and minimal moving parts made it virtually indestructible under field conditions. This reliability proved invaluable in the harsh operational environment of Northern Ireland, where weapons often required extended storage in hidden caches and immediate functionality after prolonged neglect.

Republican organisations, particularly the Provisional IRA, acquired M3 submachine guns through various sources, including American military surplus, sympathetic veterans, and international arms dealers. The weapon's .45 ACP chambering delivered substantial stopping power at close range, making it highly effective for the urban warfare scenarios typical of the conflict. Its slow, controllable rate of fire – approximately 450 rounds per minute – allowed for more accurate sustained bursts compared to higher-cycling weapons.

Loyalist paramilitaries also utilised M3s, often obtained through private collections, military surplus channels, or theft from legitimate sources. The weapon's association with Allied victory in World War II carried symbolic resonance for groups defending the Union with Britain, adding psychological weight to its practical advantages.

The M3's wire stock and compact dimensions made it relatively concealable while maintaining submachine gun effectiveness. British security forces regularly encountered these weapons during raids and post-incident investigations, with the Grease Gun's distinctive profile becoming a familiar sight in evidence photographs throughout the Troubles.

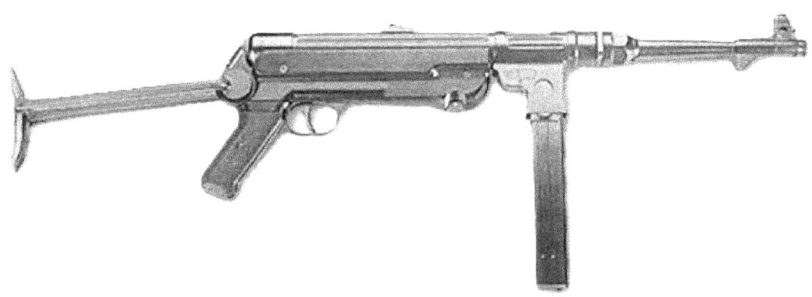

9mm MP 38/40 Submachine Gun

German Engineering in Ireland's Modern Conflict

The MP 38 and MP 40 submachine guns – iconic German weapons from World War II – maintained a haunting presence during the Troubles, representing some of the most historically charged firearms to appear in Northern Ireland's conflict. These precision-engineered weapons, synonymous with Wehrmacht infantry and SS units, carried profound symbolic weight alongside their tactical effectiveness.

The MP 40's technical superiority made it highly sought after by paramilitary organisations despite its age. Its innovative folding stock, excellent balance, and controllable 500-round-per-minute cyclic rate provided exceptional accuracy for sustained automatic fire. The weapon's robust construction and simple maintenance requirements ensured reliability even after decades of storage, making war surplus examples viable combat weapons throughout the 1970s and 1980s.

Republican groups, particularly the Provisional IRA, occasionally acquired MP 38/40s through European arms networks and war relic collectors. The weapons often arrived through the same continental smuggling routes that supplied other European military surplus, reflecting the international scope of Republican procurement operations. Their 9mm Parabellum chambering shared ammunition compatibility with various pistols and other submachine guns already in circulation.

Loyalist paramilitaries also utilised these weapons, though their acquisition posed particular ideological complications given the firearms' Nazi associations. However, tactical considerations often overrode historical sensitivities when effective automatic weapons were available. The MP 40's reputation for reliability and accuracy made it valuable regardless of its origins.

British security forces treated encounters with MP 38/40s as particularly significant, given both their combat effectiveness and historical implications. The weapons' appearance in Northern Ireland demonstrated the conflict's connection to broader European military history and the persistence of World War II-era weaponry in modern guerrilla warfare.

The psychological impact of these weapons extended beyond their tactical utility – their distinctive profile and historical associations added layers of intimidation and symbolic meaning to their deployment in Northern Ireland's streets.

9mm Steyr MPi 69 Submachine Gun

Austrian Precision in Northern Ireland's Urban Warfare

The Steyr MPi 69 submachine gun, manufactured by Steyr-Mannlicher in Austria, represented one of the more sophisticated automatic weapons that occasionally surfaced during the Troubles. This modern, well-engineered submachine gun brought contemporary European military technology to Northern Ireland's conflict through specialised arms procurement networks and international smuggling operations.

The MPi 69's appeal to paramilitary organisations lay in its advanced design features and exceptional reliability. Its innovative wraparound bolt system and telescope-style operating mechanism provided smooth, controllable automatic fire with minimal recoil and muzzle climb. The weapon's modular construction and precision manufacturing made it significantly more accurate than cruder submachine guns, offering tactical advantages in the confined urban environment of Belfast and Londonderry.

Republican groups, particularly the Provisional IRA, acquired MPi 69s through sophisticated European arms networks, often alongside other Austrian and German weapons. The submachine gun's presence reflected the evolution of Republican procurement operations toward more professional military equipment as the conflict intensified. Its 9mm Parabellum chambering maintained ammunition compatibility with existing weapon systems while delivering superior performance.

The weapon's distinctive appearance, with its unconventional bolt design and modern polymer components, made it instantly recognisable to security forces familiar with contemporary military hardware. Its relatively high manufacturing cost and limited civilian availability meant that MPi 69s in Northern Ireland typically indicated well-funded, professionally equipped paramilitary units rather than opportunistic armed groups.

Loyalist paramilitaries encountered these weapons less frequently, primarily due to their limited access to continental European arms networks compared to Republican organisations. When MPi 69s did appear in Loyalist hands, they usually indicated significant arms deals or sophisticated procurement operations beyond typical local acquisition methods.

British security forces regarded the MPi 69's presence as evidence of increasingly militarised paramilitary capabilities and international arms trafficking networks extending deep into European defence manufacturing regions.

.45 ACP Thompson Submachine Gun

American Icon in Ireland's Revolutionary War

The Thompson submachine gun – the legendary "Tommy Gun" of Prohibition-era America – held a uniquely prominent place in Northern Ireland's conflict, serving as both a practical weapon and a powerful symbol of armed resistance. This iconic American firearm, with its distinctive drum magazines and unmistakable profile, became synonymous with Republican paramilitaries and their historical connections to Irish-American support networks.

The Thompson's reputation preceded its arrival in Northern Ireland, carrying the mystique of Chicago gangsters and World War II paratroopers. Its robust .45 ACP chambering delivered devastating stopping power at close range, while its solid construction and reliable mechanism made it ideal for the demanding conditions of guerrilla warfare. The weapon's weight and substantial recoil actually aided controllability during automatic fire, allowing experienced operators to maintain accuracy during sustained engagements.

Republican organisations, particularly the Provisional IRA, acquired Thompsons primarily through Irish-American fundraising networks and sympathetic veterans. The weapon's symbolic value to Irish Republicans was immense, representing both American support for the cause and continuity with earlier generations of Irish revolutionaries who had utilised similar weapons. Fundraising events in Irish-American communities often specifically sought to purchase these weapons for "the boys back home."

The Thompson's most famous deployment occurred during high-profile IRA operations, where its distinctive appearance and sound made powerful psychological impressions. Its presence at major incidents reinforced the IRA's image as a serious military organisation rather than a mere terrorist group, contributing to their broader propaganda objectives.

Loyalist paramilitaries rarely utilised Thompsons, partly due to their limited access to Irish-American networks and partly because of the weapon's strong association with Republican identity. When Loyalists did acquire Thompsons, they typically came through different channels, such as military surplus or private collections.

British security forces treated Thompson encounters as particularly significant, recognising both the weapon's combat effectiveness and its symbolic importance to Republican morale and international perception.

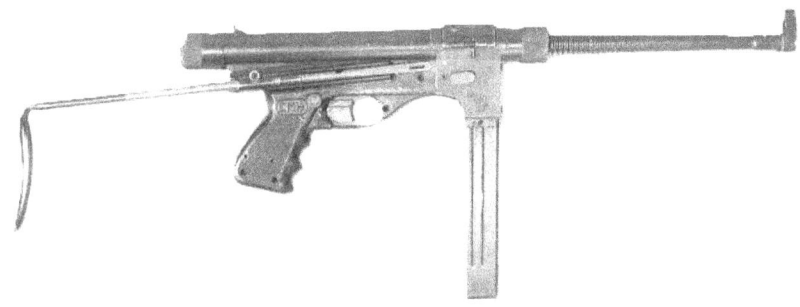

9mm Vigneron Submachine Gun

South African Engineering in Northern Ireland's Covert Operations

The Vigneron submachine gun, manufactured by Lyttleton Engineering Works in South Africa, represented one of the more unusual and sophisticated automatic weapons that occasionally appeared during the Troubles. This distinctive South African design, developed during the apartheid era, found its way into Northern Ireland through complex international arms networks that reflected the global nature of the conflict's supply chains.

The Vigneron's tactical advantages lay in its innovative design features and exceptional manufacturing quality. Its unique telescoping bolt system and precision engineering delivered remarkably smooth automatic fire with minimal recoil, making it highly controllable during sustained engagements. The weapon's distinctive appearance, with its perforated barrel shroud and angular lines, made it instantly recognisable to those familiar with contemporary military hardware.

Republican organisations, particularly the Provisional IRA, acquired Vignerons through sophisticated arms dealers operating across multiple continents. The weapon's presence in Northern Ireland demonstrated the reach of Republican procurement networks, which extended far beyond traditional European and American sources to include African and Middle Eastern suppliers. Its 9mm Parabellum chambering maintained ammunition compatibility with existing weapon systems while offering superior performance characteristics.

The submachine gun's relatively limited production numbers and specialised nature meant that their appearance in Northern Ireland typically indicated high-level arms transactions rather than opportunistic acquisitions. Security forces regarded Vigneron seizures as evidence of well-funded, professionally equipped paramilitary units with access to international defence industry contacts.

Loyalist paramilitaries encountered these weapons infrequently, primarily due to their limited connections to the international arms networks that facilitated such specialised acquisitions. The Vigneron's association with South African military forces during the apartheid era added complex political dimensions to its presence in the conflict.

British intelligence services closely monitored Vigneron appearances, recognising them as indicators of sophisticated arms trafficking operations that often involved multiple countries and criminal organisations spanning several continents.

7.62mm AK-47 Assault Rifle

Soviet Engineering in Ireland's Revolutionary Struggle

The AK-47 assault rifle – perhaps the most iconic weapon of 20th-century insurgencies – became a defining symbol of Republican paramilitaries during the Troubles, representing both formidable firepower and international solidarity with liberation movements worldwide. This legendary Soviet-designed weapon brought battlefield-grade automatic rifle capability to Northern Ireland's urban conflict, fundamentally altering the tactical landscape of the Troubles.

The AK-47's reputation for absolute reliability under adverse conditions made it ideal for paramilitary operations in Northern Ireland's harsh climate and demanding operational environment. Its robust construction, simple maintenance requirements, and ability to function despite neglect or abuse proved invaluable for weapons cached in hidden locations or subjected to prolonged field use. The rifle's 7.62x39mm cartridge delivered devastating stopping power and penetration capability far exceeding that of submachine guns or pistols.

Republican organisations, particularly the Provisional IRA, acquired AK-47s through extensive international networks that connected them to socialist governments, Palestinian liberation groups, and Libyan arms suppliers. The weapon's presence symbolised the IRA's position within the broader anti-imperialist struggle, linking their cause to revolutionary movements across Africa, Asia, and Latin America.

The psychological impact of AK-47s extended far beyond their tactical utility. Their distinctive silhouette and association with successful insurgencies worldwide made them powerful propaganda tools, appearing in Republican murals, photographs, and ceremonial displays. The weapon's presence conveyed serious military capability and international backing, enhancing the IRA's credibility as a liberation army rather than a terrorist organisation.

British security forces regarded AK-47 encounters as evidence of the conflict's escalation from localised unrest to international insurgency. The rifle's appearance triggered intensive intelligence operations to trace supply networks and prevent further acquisitions, recognising their potential to dramatically increase paramilitary effectiveness against military and police targets.

For further interesting information

[ii] See endnote.

5.56mm ArmaLite Rifle

American Technology in Republican Hands

The ArmaLite rifle – primarily the AR-15 and AR-18 variants chambered in 5.56mm NATO – became one of the most significant and symbolically powerful weapons in the Republican arsenal during the Troubles. These American-designed rifles brought modern military technology and devastating firepower to the conflict, fundamentally transforming paramilitary capabilities and becoming synonymous with IRA operations throughout the 1970s and 1980s.

The ArmaLite's tactical superiority over traditional weapons was immediately apparent to Republican operatives. Its lightweight construction, modular design, and high-velocity 5.56mm cartridge delivered exceptional accuracy and penetration at extended ranges, making it devastatingly effective against security force personnel and vehicles. The rifle's semi-automatic and selective-fire capabilities provided versatility for both precision shooting and suppressive fire, while its relatively compact size allowed for easier concealment and transport than traditional battle rifles.

Republican organisations, particularly the Provisional IRA, acquired ArmaLites primarily through Irish-American networks, with significant quantities purchased legally in the United States and smuggled across the Atlantic. The "ArmaLite and ballot box" strategy articulated by Sinn Féin leadership explicitly acknowledged the weapon's central role in Republican military thinking. These rifles often arrived alongside Thompson submachine guns and other American weapons, demonstrating the sophistication of transatlantic arms trafficking operations.

The psychological impact of ArmaLites was profound – their modern appearance and association with contemporary military forces projected an image of technological sophistication that enhanced Republican credibility. The weapon's name became shorthand for IRA military capability, appearing in songs, slogans, and political rhetoric as a symbol of armed resistance against British rule.

British security forces regarded ArmaLite proliferation as a critical threat multiplier, requiring enhanced body armour, vehicle protection, and tactical responses. The rifles' long-range accuracy and penetration capability forced significant changes in security force operations, patrol procedures, and base construction throughout Northern Ireland.

The weapon's presence in Republican hands also created diplomatic tensions between Britain and the United States, as American-manufactured rifles were being used to kill British soldiers and police officers.

For further interesting information

[iii] See endnote.

7.62mm Valmet M63/S Assault Rifle

Finnish Military Engineering in Northern Ireland's Professional Arsenal

The Valmet M63/S assault rifle – a sophisticated Finnish-manufactured weapon based on the proven AK-47 design but incorporating significant Nordic engineering improvements – emerged as a notable automatic weapon during the Troubles, bringing Scandinavian precision manufacturing and enhanced reliability to Northern Ireland's conflict through specialised European arms networks that demonstrated the truly international scope of paramilitary procurement.

The M63/S's tactical advantages lay in its superior manufacturing quality compared to standard Soviet-bloc AK variants, while maintaining the proven reliability and stopping power of the 7.62x39mm cartridge. Finnish precision engineering resulted in tighter tolerances, improved accuracy, and enhanced durability, while retaining the simple operation and rugged construction that made Kalashnikov-pattern rifles so effective in guerrilla warfare. The weapon's distinctive Finnish modifications, including improved furniture and manufacturing techniques, provided performance advantages over standard Eastern Bloc production.

Republican organisations, particularly units within the Provisional IRA seeking high-quality automatic weapons, acquired M63/S rifles through sophisticated Scandinavian arms networks that operated during the 1970s and 1980s. These weapons typically indicated extremely advanced procurement operations with access to Nordic defence industry sources, representing the pinnacle of Republican armament sophistication. The rifle's military specification and restricted availability suggested connections to professional channels typically reserved for legitimate government customers.

The weapon's Finnish origin was particularly significant as neutral Nordic countries generally maintained strict arms export controls. M63/S acquisitions were therefore indicators of either significant criminal penetration of legitimate defence industries or potential state-level involvement in Republican supply networks. British security forces regarded these seizures as evidence of the most sophisticated international arms trafficking operations supporting Republican activities.

Loyalist paramilitaries virtually never encountered these weapons, primarily due to their extremely limited availability and the specialised Nordic networks required for acquisition. The M63/S's appearance in Northern Ireland almost exclusively indicated Republican procurement through the most advanced international channels available to paramilitary organisations.

The rifle's exceptional build quality and precision manufacturing ensured consistent performance even after extended storage in harsh conditions, making it highly valued by Republican operatives familiar with its superior characteristics compared to standard Eastern Bloc weapons.

For further interesting information

[iv] See endnote.

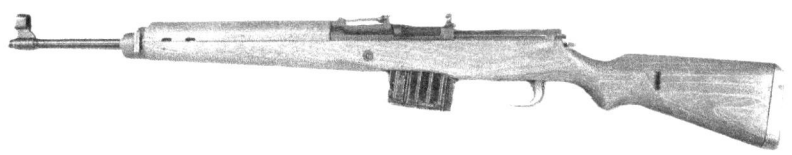

7.92mm Gewehr 43 Semi-Automatic Rifle

German Wartime Engineering in Northern Ireland's Historical Arsenal

The Gewehr 43 semi-automatic rifle – an advanced German weapon developed during World War II as an improvement over the earlier G41 design – appeared occasionally during the Troubles as a distinctive piece of military history turned toward contemporary conflict.

This gas-operated rifle brought proven Germanic engineering and powerful 7.92x57mm Mauser cartridge performance to Northern Ireland, representing both the enduring utility of wartime weaponry and the complex historical layers underlying the Province's armed struggle.

The G43's tactical advantages lay in its semi-automatic operation combined with the devastating 7.92mm Mauser cartridge that delivered exceptional long-range accuracy and stopping power. Its ten-round detachable magazine provided superior sustained fire capability compared to bolt-action rifles, while its proven combat record from the Eastern Front demonstrated reliability under demanding conditions. The weapon's precision manufacturing and robust construction ensured consistent performance decades after production ended.

Republican organisations, particularly historically-minded units within the Provisional IRA, acquired G43s through European military surplus networks and private collectors fascinated by World War II weaponry. These rifles often carried significant symbolic weight, representing European resistance against occupying forces – a parallel that Republican propagandists readily exploited. The weapon's scarcity and historical significance made each acquisition noteworthy within Republican armament circles.

The rifle's German origin and World War II pedigree created complex psychological dynamics for both operators and targets. While some Republican operatives appreciated its engineering excellence and proven combat effectiveness, others remained uncomfortable with weapons associated with Nazi Germany, despite their technical merits. British security forces recognised the G43's historical significance while treating it as a serious tactical threat due to its accuracy and power.

Loyalist paramilitaries rarely encountered these weapons, primarily due to their limited availability and the specialised collector networks typically required for acquisition. When G43s did appear in Loyalist hands, they usually indicated connections to military history enthusiasts or unusual procurement circumstances rather than systematic armament programs.

The weapon's distinctive appearance and powerful cartridge made it immediately recognisable to security forces familiar with World War II weaponry, often triggering investigations into military surplus networks and private collections throughout Europe.

For further interesting information

[v] See endnote.

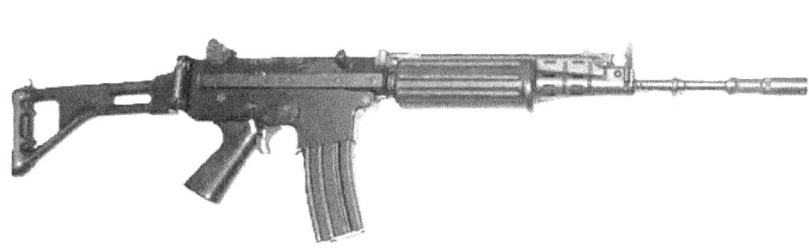

5.56mm FN FNC 2000 Assault Rifle

Belgian Innovation in Northern Ireland's Advanced Operations

The FN FNC 2000 assault rifle – a sophisticated Belgian-designed weapon manufactured by Fabrique Nationale – represented cutting-edge military technology when it occasionally surfaced during the later stages of the Troubles. This advanced assault rifle brought state-of-the-art firepower and precision to Northern Ireland's conflict, reflecting the evolution of paramilitary procurement toward increasingly professional military equipment.

The FNC 2000's appeal lay in its exceptional accuracy, reliability, and modern design features. Its 5.56mm NATO chambering delivered high-velocity performance with manageable recoil, while its precision manufacturing and advanced metallurgy ensured consistent performance under demanding operational conditions. The rifle's modular construction allowed for various configurations, including different barrel lengths and accessory mounting systems, making it adaptable to diverse tactical requirements.

Republican organisations, particularly elements within the Provisional IRA seeking to modernise their arsenal, acquired FNC 2000s through sophisticated European arms networks operating in the 1980s and early 1990s. These weapons typically indicated high-level procurement operations with access to contemporary military suppliers, representing a significant escalation from earlier, more rudimentary armament. The rifle's NATO standard ammunition maintained compatibility with other 5.56mm weapons while offering superior performance characteristics.

The weapon's appearance in Northern Ireland demonstrated the global reach of advanced arms trafficking networks and the increasing militarisation of paramilitary organisations as the conflict evolved. Its relatively high cost and limited availability meant that FNC 2000s were typically equipped by elite operational units rather than general paramilitary personnel, indicating strategic weapon allocation by sophisticated command structures.

British security forces regarded FNC 2000 encounters as evidence of highly professional paramilitary capabilities and advanced international procurement networks. The rifle's modern design and military pedigree suggested access to defence industry sources typically reserved for legitimate government customers, raising concerns about security breaches within European military supply chains.

Loyalist paramilitaries rarely encountered these weapons, primarily due to their limited access to the specialised European arms networks that facilitated such advanced acquisitions.

.50 BMG M82 Anti-Materiel Rifle

American Precision Power in Northern Ireland's Sniper War

The Barrett M82 anti-materiel rifle – the legendary .50 calibre semi-automatic weapon designed by Ronnie Barrett in Tennessee – represented the absolute pinnacle of long-range precision firepower to appear during the Troubles, fundamentally transforming the tactical landscape of Northern Ireland's conflict. This devastating American-designed rifle brought battlefield-level anti-materiel capability and unprecedented accuracy to paramilitary operations, demonstrating the extraordinary reach of international arms procurement networks.

The M82's overwhelming tactical superiority was immediately apparent in the Northern Irish context. Its .50 BMG cartridge could penetrate armoured vehicles, destroy equipment, and engage targets at ranges exceeding 1,500 metres with devastating precision. The rifle's semi-automatic capability allowed for rapid follow-up shots, while its exceptional accuracy made it ideal for both anti-personnel and anti-materiel operations. The weapon's psychological impact was immense – its distinctive report and massive muzzle blast created terror effects far beyond its physical damage capability.

Republican organisations, particularly elite sniper units within the Provisional IRA, acquired M82s through sophisticated American networks involving Irish-American sympathisers and criminal organisations with access to cutting-edge military equipment. These weapons represented the highest levels of external support and procurement sophistication, indicating quantum leaps in capability that required specialised training and extensive logistical support for effective deployment.

The rifle's American origin carried profound symbolic weight, demonstrating Republican access to the most advanced military technology available while paradoxically using American weapons against British forces allied to the United States. This contradiction created complex political dynamics that Republican propagandists exploited to demonstrate international support for their cause.

British security forces treated M82 encounters as critical strategic threats requiring immediate intelligence responses and comprehensive tactical countermeasures. The weapon's extreme range and armour-penetrating capability rendered existing protective measures obsolete, forcing fundamental changes in patrol procedures, base design, and aircraft operations throughout Northern Ireland. M82 attacks triggered major security operations to locate and neutralise these strategic weapons.

The weapon's substantial size and specialised ammunition requirements necessitated careful operational planning, often limiting deployment to major operations where its exceptional capabilities justified the logistical burden and security risks.

For further interesting information

[vi] See endnote.

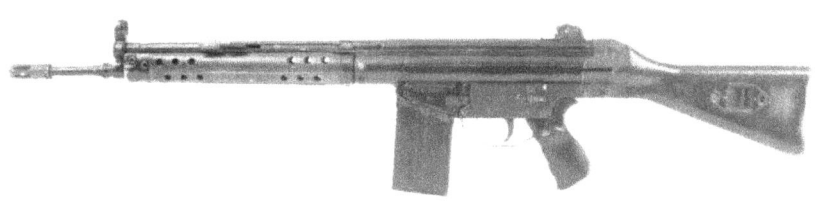

7.62mm Heckler & Koch G3 Rifle

German Precision in Northern Ireland's Escalated Conflict

The Heckler & Koch G3 battle rifle – a sophisticated German-designed weapon chambered in 7.62x51mm NATO – represented one of the most formidable firearms to appear in Northern Ireland during the Troubles. This precision-engineered rifle brought contemporary military-grade firepower and exceptional long-range capability to the conflict, significantly escalating the lethality of paramilitary operations and demonstrating access to professional military equipment.

The G3's tactical superiority was immediately apparent to paramilitary organisations familiar with its capabilities. Its powerful 7.62mm NATO cartridge delivered devastating stopping power and armour penetration at extended ranges, while the rifle's delayed blowback operating system provided reliable semi-automatic and selective-fire performance. The weapon's precision manufacturing and robust construction ensured consistent accuracy even under demanding field conditions, making it exceptionally effective for both precision shooting and sustained engagements.

Republican groups, particularly elite units within the Provisional IRA, acquired G3 rifles through sophisticated European arms networks, often alongside other German and Austrian weapons. These acquisitions typically indicated high-level procurement operations with access to military surplus or defence industry sources, representing a significant escalation from earlier, more rudimentary armament. The rifle's NATO standard ammunition maintained compatibility with other military weapons while offering superior ballistic performance.

The G3's appearance in Republican hands carried a particular psychological impact due to its association with professional military forces worldwide. Its modern design and advanced engineering projected an image of technological sophistication that enhanced Republican credibility as a serious military organisation rather than an amateur insurgent group. The weapon's presence often indicated planned operations requiring long-range precision or engagement of heavily protected targets.

British security forces regarded G3 encounters as evidence of highly militarised paramilitary capabilities and professional arms procurement networks. The rifle's military pedigree and restricted availability suggested access to defence industry channels typically reserved for legitimate government customers, raising significant intelligence concerns about European arms trafficking operations.

Loyalist paramilitaries rarely encountered these weapons, primarily due to their limited access to the specialised international networks that facilitated such advanced military acquisitions.

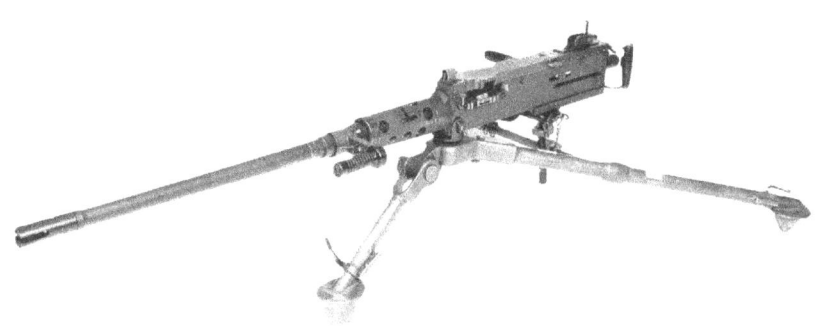

.50 Caliber Browning M2 Heavy Machine Gun

American Heavy Firepower in Northern Ireland's Escalated Warfare

The Browning M2 50 calibre heavy machine gun – one of the most devastating crew-served weapons of the 20th century – represented the absolute pinnacle of firepower available to paramilitary forces during the Troubles. This legendary American-designed weapon brought battlefield-level destructive capability to Northern Ireland's conflict, fundamentally altering the tactical landscape and demonstrating the extraordinary reach of international arms procurement networks.

The M2's overwhelming firepower made it a game-changing weapon in the Northern Irish context. Its .50 BMG cartridge could penetrate armoured vehicles, destroy aircraft, and engage targets at ranges exceeding one kilometre with devastating effect. The weapon's sustained fire capability and armour-piercing ammunition posed unprecedented threats to British security forces, requiring complete tactical reassessment of patrol procedures, base security, and vehicle protection throughout the province.

Republican organisations, particularly specialised units within the Provisional IRA, acquired M2 heavy machine guns through extraordinarily sophisticated arms networks, often involving state sponsors and international criminal organisations. These weapons typically indicated the highest levels of external support and professional military planning, representing quantum leaps in capability beyond small arms and explosives. The logistical requirements for .50 calibre ammunition and the weapon's substantial weight necessitated careful operational planning and secure transportation networks.

The psychological impact of M2 deployments was immense, demonstrating Republican capability to engage British forces with weapons typically associated with conventional military units. The heavy machine gun's appearance in Republican propaganda and operational planning projected an image of near-military parity that enhanced their political credibility and international standing as a liberation army rather than a terrorist organisation.

British security forces treated M2 encounters as critical incidents requiring immediate intelligence responses and tactical countermeasures. The weapon's range and penetration capability forced fundamental changes in base design, patrol procedures, and aircraft operations throughout Northern Ireland. Its presence often triggered major security operations to locate and neutralise these strategic weapons before deployment.

The extreme rarity of these weapons in paramilitary hands meant that each acquisition represented significant intelligence opportunities for security forces seeking to disrupt high-level arms trafficking networks.

For further interesting information

[vii] See endnote.

9mm Uzi Submachine Gun

Israeli Innovation in Northern Ireland's Urban Warfare

The Uzi submachine gun – the compact, blowback-operated weapon designed by Major Uziel Gal for the Israeli Defence Forces – became a highly significant automatic weapon during the Troubles, bringing proven combat effectiveness and exceptional reliability to Northern Ireland's conflict. This distinctive Israeli design represented sophisticated international procurement networks and demonstrated the global reach of arms trafficking that supplied the decades-long violence.

The Uzi's tactical superiority lay in its exceptional compactness combined with devastating firepower. Its telescoping bolt design minimised overall length while maintaining a full-length barrel, creating an ideal weapon for urban combat and vehicle operations. The 9mm Parabellum chambering provided excellent stopping power with manageable recoil, while its simple blowback operation ensured reliable function under adverse conditions. The weapon's high rate of fire and large magazine capacity made it devastatingly effective in close-quarters engagements.

Republican organisations, particularly elite units within the Provisional IRA, acquired Uzis through sophisticated international arms networks that often involved Middle Eastern connections and criminal organisations operating across multiple continents. These weapons typically indicated high-level procurement operations with access to military surplus or defence industry sources, representing significant escalations from earlier, more rudimentary armament. The Uzi's association with professional military forces enhanced Republican credibility as a serious armed organisation.

The weapon's Israeli origin carried complex political implications during a period when Middle Eastern conflicts and Palestinian liberation movements influenced Republican strategic thinking. Some Republican factions viewed Israeli military technology with ambivalence due to solidarity with Palestinian causes, while others appreciated the weapon's proven combat effectiveness regardless of its origins.

British security forces regarded Uzi encounters as evidence of highly sophisticated arms procurement networks and professional military capabilities within Republican organisations. The weapon's military pedigree and restricted availability suggested access to defence industry channels typically reserved for legitimate government customers, raising significant intelligence concerns about international arms trafficking operations.

Loyalist paramilitaries rarely encountered these weapons, primarily due to their limited access to the specialised international networks that facilitated such advanced military acquisitions. The Uzi's high cost and sophisticated procurement requirements typically limited its distribution to well-funded, professionally organised units.

7.62mm M60 Machine Gun

American Battlefield Technology in Northern Ireland's Urban War

The M60 machine gun – the iconic "Pig" of American forces in Vietnam – brought devastating squad-level firepower to Northern Ireland's conflict when it occasionally appeared in paramilitary hands during the Troubles. This gas-operated, belt-fed weapon represented a significant escalation in Republican military capability, providing sustained automatic fire with the powerful 7.62x51mm NATO cartridge that fundamentally altered tactical considerations for both paramilitaries and security forces.

The M60's tactical advantages were immediately apparent in the Northern Irish context. Its sustained fire capability and 7.62mm NATO chambering delivered devastating suppressive fire that could pin down security force patrols, while its bipod and relatively portable design made it suitable for ambush operations in both urban and rural environments. The weapon's belt-fed system allowed for continuous fire, limited only by ammunition supply and barrel overheating, providing capabilities far exceeding those of assault rifles or submachine guns.

Republican organisations, particularly elite units within the Provisional IRA, acquired M60s through sophisticated American networks, often involving Vietnam veterans sympathetic to the Republican cause or criminal organisations with access to military surplus. These weapons typically indicated the highest levels of procurement sophistication and external support, representing quantum leaps in capability that required specialised training and logistical support for effective deployment.

The psychological impact of M60 deployments extended far beyond their tactical utility. The weapon's association with American military forces and its distinctive sound created powerful propaganda opportunities for Republican organisations seeking to project military legitimacy. Its presence in Republican hands demonstrated access to contemporary military equipment typically reserved for professional armed forces, enhancing their credibility as a liberation army rather than an insurgent group.

British security forces regarded M60 encounters as critical incidents requiring immediate tactical responses and intelligence operations. The weapon's sustained fire capability and armour penetration posed unprecedented threats to patrol vehicles and installations, forcing significant changes in operational procedures and protective measures throughout Northern Ireland.

The weapon's substantial weight and ammunition requirements necessitated careful operational planning, often limiting its deployment to prepared positions or major operations where its firepower advantages justified the logistical burden.

For further interesting information

[viii] See endnote.

RPG-7V Rocket-Propelled Grenade Launcher

Soviet Anti-Tank Power in Northern Ireland's Asymmetric War

The RPG-7V rocket-propelled grenade launcher – the ubiquitous Soviet-designed anti-tank weapon that became synonymous with insurgencies worldwide – represented the most devastating single-shot weapon system to appear in Northern Ireland during the Troubles. This shoulder-fired launcher brought battlefield-level anti-armour capability to the conflict, fundamentally transforming paramilitary tactics and forcing comprehensive changes in British security force operations throughout the province.

The RPG-7V's tactical impact was revolutionary in the Northern Irish context. Its HEAT (High Explosive Anti-Tank) warheads could penetrate armoured vehicles, destroy fortifications, and create devastating psychological effects that extended far beyond physical damage. The weapon's relatively simple operation and robust construction made it ideal for guerrilla warfare, while its reusable launcher system allowed sustained operations with readily available ammunition supplies from international sources.

Although Loyalist organisations acquired this weapon, the Provisional IRA had substantially more of them, as they were able to obtain them through extensive international networks connecting them to Palestinian liberation groups, Libyan state sponsors, and Soviet-aligned governments worldwide. These weapons arrived alongside significant quantities of ammunition and often included training support from experienced operators. The launcher's presence indicated the highest levels of external military assistance and represented quantum leaps in anti-vehicle capability.

The psychological impact of RPG deployments was immense, demonstrating Republican capability to engage British armoured vehicles and installations with weapons typically associated with conventional military forces. Successful RPG attacks against security force targets created powerful propaganda victories while forcing fundamental tactical changes in patrol procedures, base design, and vehicle protection throughout Northern Ireland.

British security forces treated RPG encounters as critical strategic threats requiring immediate intelligence responses and tactical countermeasures. The weapon's armour-penetrating capability rendered many existing protective measures obsolete, forcing rapid deployment of enhanced armour systems and completely revised operational procedures. RPG attacks often triggered major security operations to locate and neutralise these strategic weapons before further deployment.

The weapon's relatively compact size and simple operation made it suitable for urban ambushes, while its devastating effectiveness against both armoured and soft targets made every successful attack a significant tactical and propaganda victory for Republican forces.

For further interesting information

[ix] See endnote

A Message from Our Heart to Yours

The stories you have just read – of courage under fire, of ordinary people in extraordinary circumstances, of truth emerging from chaos – represent precisely what we are fighting to preserve.

But time is running out

Whilst you turned these pages, witnesses to similar untold stories grew older. Their memories fade. Their voices weaken. And with each passing day, pieces of Northern Ireland's true history disappear forever. For some, we have fulfilled their last desire by recording the story of their loved one.

Join Heritage Guardians

What We Do

We race against time to capture the unfiltered testimonies that politicians, academics, and revisionist historians prefer to ignore. Like the accounts in this book, we preserve truth – not convenient narratives.

Our current projects include:

1. Recording final testimonies from ageing witnesses

2. Digitally preserving family archives before they are lost

3. Publishing suppressed accounts

4. Creating documentaries that let witnesses speak for themselves

Why This Matters to You

If our stories move you, it is because authentic voices cut through decades of propaganda. We ensure future generations will have access to equally powerful, unvarnished accounts – before the last witnesses are silenced by time.

The Reality

Each week, we have key witnesses whose stories have never been recorded contacting us. Twenty-three are over 80. Several are in declining health.

For £20 per month or more it will help us record stories for our future generations.

As a Heritage Guardian, you will receive:

1. Exclusive access to unpublished testimonies and interviews

2. Insights into the scenes

3. Invites to our events

4. Updates with excerpts from our latest discoveries

5. 20% discount on all publications and events

Contact us:

Email: info@MauriceWylieMedia.com

The stories in "The Red Caps" survived because someone cared enough to preserve them. Now it is your turn to ensure other crucial testimonies do not vanish into silence.

Become a Heritage Guardian. The key witnesses are waiting.

Scan me

The Book that Launched the Recording of these Stories

WHEN TIME IS TAKEN

by

NORAH BRADFORD

Bestseller

REVIEW

"This is a heartbreaking yet essential read that strips away the sanitised political narratives about Northern Ireland's Troubles. The author doesn't pull any punches describing how ordinary families like Robert and Norah's lived under constant threat - bulletproof glass, checking cars for bombs, even planning picnics around security concerns. What makes this particularly powerful is how it shows the human cost behind the headlines, especially that devastating final scene where terrorists murdered Robert in front of children at a birthday party. The writing is raw and honest, clearly coming from someone who lived through this nightmare rather than observed it from afar. Most importantly, it doesn't let anyone off the hook - not just the killers, but the governments who colluded and covered up the truth. A gripping, necessary book that deserves to be read by anyone wanting to understand what really happened during those dark years."

Look inside

In war-torn Northern Ireland, Norah and Robert's love flourished amidst terrorism's menacing grip. Robert, a Methodist Minister, and Norah, an SRN at the Royal Victoria Hospital, Belfast, embraced parenthood with adoption. However, threats loomed as republican terrorists targeted Robert, now an MP. Tragedy struck when terrorists hid themselves behind children and pensioners, callously executing Robert in cold blood, tearing Norah's world apart.

In "When Time is Taken," Norah's voice resounds against deception and treachery. Her fight transcends those who stole her husband's life, exposing colluding governments and hidden evidence.

This gripping true story unveils Norah's unwavering resilience, the strength forged amidst grief, and her relentless pursuit of justice. With indomitable determination, she demands truth, refusing to be silenced by the darkness that seeks to smother victims' voices from revealing the truth.

The First Book of the Truth Revealed Series...

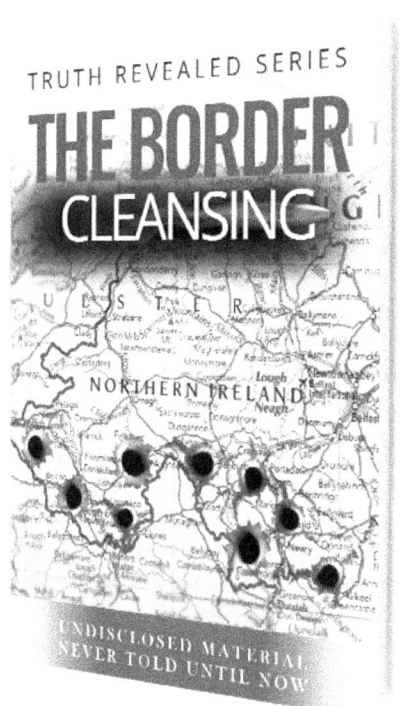

Endorsed by Alan Black, (shot 18 times) sole survivor of the Kingsmill Massacre

Bestseller

REVIEW

"What sets this book apart from other accounts of the period is its unflinching focus on the personal cost of sectarian violence. Rather than political analysis or strategic overview, readers are confronted with the raw, unfiltered experiences of survivors and families who lived through unimaginable horror. The inclusion of previously untold stories—such as the chilling account of a second bomb at Enniskillen and the twelve-year-old boy who faced his father's killer—provides crucial missing pieces to our understanding of this period.

These are not secondhand accounts or academic interpretations, but firsthand testimonies from those who were there. The endorsement by Alan Black, himself a survivor of the Kingsmill Massacre, lends additional weight to the credibility of these accounts. The authors have clearly taken great care to preserve the voices of the victims while ensuring their stories are told with dignity and respect."

Look inside

In this heart-wrenching collection of true stories, readers are taken on a journey through the brutal reality of life in the border areas between Northern Ireland and the Republic of Ireland. With unflinching honesty and raw emotion, the survivors of these horrific atrocities share their stories of pain, loss, and grief.

Learn the full truth of the Kingsmill Massacre as told by the daughters of one of the ten victims, endorsed by Alan Black, who was shot eighteen times and survived; the untold story of the bomb that was set to explode 20 minutes after the Enniskillen bomb and of the children who stood beside it while terrorists watched nearby; the twelve-year-old boy who looked into the eyes of his father's murderer; the dog lovers who were ambushed and killed in cold blood; the Christian fellowship that was surrounded and attacked as they worshipped; plus others. These stories will shock, horrify, and move readers to tears.

Find out the names and backgrounds of the individuals who were murdered in cold blood along the borders of Counties Down, Armagh, and Fermanagh.

If only these events along the border had never taken place, lives would have been spared, and over five hundred children would not have lost a parent; farmers would still have their land; the miscarriage of justice and cover-ups would never have happened, and those seeking to rewrite history would not have cause to do so.

With a powerful narrative and compelling characters, this is a must-read for anyone interested in the history of Ireland and the ongoing struggle that endures even to this day for peace in the region. Secrets, lies, cover-ups, and the slaughter of the innocent, as told by those who were there during The Border Cleansing.

Amazon Rating

Review (Condensed)

"I've just finished reading this book! It was compelling reading and very well written. The scene was set perfectly, and any aspect the reader would not be expected to understand was explained, giving us access to "inside knowledge".

It is terrifying to think happenings like these were going on not only in Springfield but in many other RUC stations and towns across the province for so many years.

I felt I was in Bravo Delta Eight Zero each time it drove out through the gates. Or in the car being tailed. Or in the station reception when the bomb was thrown in. The fear on these occasions, but also the amazingly calm presence of mind, and sheer bravery, were palpable. Rescuing a family from a burning house; being blown off your feet by a blast bomb and reporting back for duty the very next night. Hero doesn't come close to describing someone who can do that!

Details were included that we would never imagine, like being shuttled in and out of the barracks when coming on and off duty, having to change your route home every day, going to somewhere safe for hot food occasionally, as you couldn't simply drive up to a regular cafe. Then there was the dark humour, making light of very grave situations as a way of coping.

The author has done the serving officers of the RUC proud in documenting these stories for all time. Everyone in Northern Ireland who lived through the troubles should read this book - we are all indebted to the author and his colleagues more than we'll ever know.

A good book leaves a lasting impact and a feeling of being there in the story with the characters. I give this book 10 out of 10 for that reason!"

Look inside

Learn what it was like to be in the RUC during the Northern Ireland Troubles. Delve into the harrowing experiences of police officers stationed at Springfield Road Station, which was situated in the heartland of Republican terrorists in Belfast. This compelling narrative exposes the daily dangers faced by those who served there, where the threat of violence was so pervasive that a sign was erected inside the main entrance gates to remind officers not to stand behind them, as terrorists often fired 'blindly' at the gate area.

What was it like to be under threat 24/7? How did officers cope with coded callsigns, ambushes, sniper fire, mortar bombs, and murder? This book reveals the gritty reality of their existence, including the time when one officer was inadvertently stranded on the Falls Road, and the heroic story of a soldier who gave his life to save a local family from death.

Through private accounts and personal stories, this book offers a raw and unfiltered look at the lives of the brave men and women who worked out of this besieged base. From the constant threat of death to the psychological toll of serving in such a volatile environment, this book provides a poignant and powerful testament to their resilience and courage.

Discover the untold stories where every day was a battle for survival and every officer was a hero in **Without Fear or Favour.**

Review

"This book is a powerful collection of testimonies from Christian men and women who endured the darkest days of the Northern Ireland Troubles. Through deeply personal accounts of loss, resilience, and faith, Marcus captures not only the pain of violence but also the hope found in Christ amid suffering. From families targeted by terrorists to children left bereaved, each story is told with honesty and compassion, reminding us of the cost of conflict and the sustaining power of faith. A moving and thought-provoking read that preserves voices which must never be forgotten."

Look inside

It was over twenty-one years ago that Marcus and his wife Pat arrived on the shores of Northern Ireland and it wasn't long before they found out — it was very difficult to travel anywhere in Northern Ireland without meeting a family who had never been affected by the Troubles. Such was the reach of the conflict.

At the centre of the book are stories of Christian people who suffered traumatic events during the years of the Troubles. Woven into the telling of these precious stories is the message of Christian suffering and its place in our lives.

Stories include…

Rodney Wilson
– Mountain Lodge Massacre.

Paul Elliott
– A Christian family targeted by terrorists.

Sara-Louise Martin
– Daughter of Inspector Martin who was murdered.

Maggie Burrows
– Brother-in-law murdered – Herbie Burrows.

David Clements
– He tells the story of his dad's murder – Billy Clements.

TO PURCHASE THESE BOOKS, VISIT

www.MauriceWylieMedia.com

Specialist in Life Stories

www.TruthRevealedSeries.com

(Research Team)

DO YOU HAVE A STORY FROM THE TROUBLES?

or

INSPIRED TO WRITE A BOOK?

WE WOULD LOVE TO HEAR FROM YOU.

Contact

Maurice Wylie Media

Your Inspirational Book Publisher

Based in Northern Ireland and distributing around the world

www.MauriceWylieMedia.com

Endnotes

[i] The traditional and original spelling associated with the family and their landholdings in Belfast, dating back to the city's early history, is Donegall with two "L"s. This is because the place is named after the Donegall family, who held titles as Earls and Marquesses of Donegall.

[ii] Loaded .303 rifles found by Irish security forces at an IRA training camp in Kilkelly, County Mayo, as late as 1985: Lee-Enfield reportedly still in active use in sniper role in late 1980s.

[iii] Small numbers were reported in the IRA inventory by 1976. Several attempts at importing from the Middle East and the United States were foiled in the 1970s. Used in attacks and at training camps since 1983. Colonel Gaddafi's Libya became a particularly significant source, with large shipments arriving via covert maritime operations from 1985, of which 1,000 rifles were seized by French security forces aboard the Libyan arms freighter Eksund in 1987. IRA was believed to still have approximately 650 AK-47/AKM rifles in inventory in 1992.

[iv] George Harrison, born in County Mayo, would later emigrate to New York in the early 1940s, where in 1944, he joined the US Army. As a strong supporter of Sinn Féin, he was asked if he would be able to source arms for the IRA. This he did through George de Meo, an Italian-American neighbour of his who had connections to the Mafia as well as gun runners who were supplying rebels in Cuba. In 1981, Harrison was arrested by the FBI Joint Terrorism Task Force during a sting operation called "Operation Bushmill." Although he had spent much of the previous decade involved in this operation, his acquittal marked the end of his active career as an IRA gun-runner as well as

the IRA's considerable source of American arms supply. He died at the age of 89 in October 2004 from natural causes at his home in Brooklyn, New York City.

[v] A British soldier came across a woman in the Ardoyne area of Belfast in 1976 who had in her possession a 7.62mm Valmet. The serial number traced the rifle to Harrison Network (See note iv).

[vi] Irish security forces under a number of them at Buncrana in County Donegal in 1976. The serial number traced them to Harrison Network. The IRA used them at their training camp in 1983.

[vii] In August 1986, the second M82 had been sent in pieces from Chicago to Dublin, where the rifle was reassembled. It was part of a batch of two sold to Michael Suárez, a Cuban resident of Cleveland, on 27 January 1995 by a firearms dealer. Suárez later passed the weapons to an Irishman, who finally shipped the rifles, their ammunition and two telescopic sights to the Republic of Ireland.

The South Armagh Sniper was made up of two IRA units, one responsible for the east part of South Armagh, the other for the west. The volunteer in charge of the Cullyhanna unit was Frank "One Shot" McCabe, a senior IRA member from Crossmaglen. Each team comprised at least four members, not counting those in charge of support activities, such as scouting for targets and driving vehicles. Military officials claim that the Dromintee-based squad deployed up to 20 volunteers in some of the sniping missions.

After two attacks in 1997, a Special Air Service (SAS) unit captured four men from the sniper team based in the west of the region on 10 April, who were responsible for several deaths. James McArdle, Michael Caraher, Bernard McGinn and Martin Mines were seized at a farm near Freeduff, Crossmaglen, South Armagh, and handed over to the RUC. The British troops were under strict orders to avoid IRA casualties. A Barrett M90 rifle was seized. It was suspected that an IRA informer, the Officer Commanding (OC), gave the snipers" location to his handler.

Irish Independent

> By the time of the final IRA ceasefire in August 1997, the South Armagh IRA leadership was already heavily involved in fuel and cigarette smuggling and it is believed that the British struck a deal whereby the IRA leaders could continue to benefit from the illicit trade, so long as no further attacks on security forces or bomb attacks on commercial targets took place.
>
> From that point onwards, the South Armagh "OC" and his associates became millionaires while continuing to donate a reputed 25pc of their earnings to the "movement". The "OC" is said to have bought another substantial portion of farmland in Armagh.

The capture of the sniper unit was the greatest success for the security forces in South Armagh in more than a decade. The men were set free 18 months later, under the terms of the Good Friday Agreement. The Dromintee sniper party has not been apprehended yet.

[viii] First publicly displayed by the IRA in 1977. IRA is believed to have smuggled at least two examples into Ireland and used them in several attacks on British helicopters in the 1980s. One was uncovered with ammunition by security forces in an IRA arms dump in West Belfast in 1986.

[ix] Six M60s and forty-six M16s were stolen in a raid on the National Guard armoury in Danvers, in August 1976 by the Irish and Italian mafias and purchased by the Harrison Network. Five M60s arrived in Ireland in late 1977, with the sixth delayed to 1979. Two more M60s were seized by police in a large weapons shipment at Dublin port in 1979.

[x] 25 launchers and 496 warheads were smuggled to Ireland from Libya in late 1972 and further shipments from Libya in 1985-1987. An attempted import from Lebanon was intercepted in Antwerp in 1977. First used in 1972, with nearly two hundred attacks involving the RPG-7 recorded by 1981. The IRA was believed to still have upwards of 40 launchers in inventory in 1992.

www.ingramcontent.com/pod-product-compliance
Lightning Source LLC
Chambersburg PA
CBHW052013070526
44584CB00016B/1739